AN
ISLAND
ODYSSEY

AN
ISLAND
ODYSSEY

HAMISH HASWELL-SMITH

CANONGATE
Edinburgh · London

This paperback edition published in 2014

First published in Great Britain in 1999
by Canongate Books Ltd
14 High Street
Edinburgh EH1 1TE

1

Contents based on the 'Island of the Week' series by Hamish Haswell-Smith
published in *The Herald*

British Library Cataloguing-in-Publication Data
A catalogue record for this book is available on request from the British Library

ISBN 978 1 78211 175 7

Design: Janet Jamieson

frontispiece: Goat Island anchorage by Eilean Righ

Printed and bound in China by Toppan Leefung

To *Jandara*,
and all who sail in her.

Goat Island anchorage by Eilean Righ

Contents

It is a piece of weakness and folly merely to value things because of the distance from the place where we are born: thus men have travelled far enough in the search of foreign plants and animals, and yet continue strangers to those produced in their own natural climate.

Martin Martin 1698

Preface

It began with Gavin Bell – that lean and rangy foreign correspondent and author of the award-winning book *In Search of Tusitola*, which is an intriguing account of his travels among the many islands of the Pacific on the trail of Robert Louis Stevenson. He suggested to Cate Devine, the vivacious editor of the *Herald* weekly magazine, that I should write a series of articles: each one about a different Scottish island, selected at random and illustrated with an original watercolour, mainly factual, but leavened with an occasional local myth or personal anecdote. I succumbed and this book is the response to many readers' requests that the series, which initially ran for a year, should be published in a more permanent form.

For the purpose of coherence, I have rearranged the articles so that they follow an imaginary voyage of discovery, an odyssey. This has one shortcoming. Because the articles refer in fact to separate visits at different times and my sailing companions also vary there is an occasional lack of what film-makers call 'continuity'. I hope the reader will forgive this.

Of the many close friends who sail with me I have a special bond with Peter, Ian and Craig through our joint ownership of *Jandara*, our well-bred sloop-rigged Moody 41. This remarkably amicable partnership has given us many memorable voyages of discovery together. Among the others I must mention are Harry and Brenda who have sailed with me for many years; with Harry's sailing ability and Brenda's expertise in the galley they are an asset to any cruise; and my cousin Ronald, yet another competent sailor and amusing raconteur. There are, of course, many more who have sailed in *Jandara* either with me or my partners and we have much to thank them for because each and every one of them has contributed something of interest to the sea-chest full of memories which *Jandara* carries with her.

I have strung the islands on a thread of abridged quotations from the inimitable Martin Martin. We all owe a debt to him, because anyone carrying out historical research on the Scottish islands soon comes across his remarkable book, published in 1703,★ which recorded so much of interest for posterity. The full title, which gives some conception of its wide scope, is:

'A Description of the Western Islands of SCOTLAND containing

'A Full Account of their Situation, Extent, Soils, Product, Harbours, Bays, Tides, Anchoring Places, and Fisheries.

★ The 1703 edition was recently reprinted by Birlinn Ltd of Edinburgh.

'The Ancient and Modern Government, Religion and Customs of the Inhabitants, particularly of their Druids, Heathen Temples, Monasteries, Churches, Chappels, Antiquities, Monuments, Forts, Caves, and other Curiosities of Art and Nature.
Of their Admirable and Expeditious way of Curing most Diseases by Simples of their own Product.
'A Particular Account of the *Second Sight*, or Faculty of foreseeing things to come, by way of Vision, so common among them.
'A Brief Hint of Methods to Improve Trade in that Country, both by Sea and Land.
'With a New MAP of the whole, describing the Harbours, Anchoring Places, and dangerous Rocks, for the benefit of Sailers.
'To which is added a Brief Description of the Isles of Orkney, and Schetland.
By M.MARTIN Gent.'

Apart from a very brief appraisal of the 'Hybrides' by Dean Sir Donald Munro in 1549 (and not published until 1774) Martin was the first person ever to write a comprehensive account of this wonderful region. At the time his book was published the area was almost entirely inaccessible and unknown and the average mainlander then knew less about the Scottish islands than the average mainlander of today knows about, say, the tribes of central Papua New Guinea.

BUT WHO WAS MARTIN MARTIN?

He was born in about 1657 near Duntulm at the northern tip of Skye. His family had a sea-faring background for his great-grandfather had roamed the Western Isles, master of his own galley, and known to his contemporaries as Angus of the Wind (Aonghas na Gaoithe). He was said to have married a Danish princess. Martin's father, Donald, fought under the Macdonald banner in the Montrose campaign, became a chamberlain of Troternish and married the niece of Sir Donald Macdonald of Sleat. Martin was his third or fourth son – the youngest. When he was about twenty-four years old he graduated MA at Edinburgh University and became a tutor, first to the young Laird Macdonald, and later to MacLeod of Dunvegan.

Then in 1692, Sir Robert Sibbald, the antiquary, asked him if he would collect information on the conditions and habits of the islanders and it was this request that set him on a course which changed his life. As an educated man with an enquiring mind, an islander who was at home in the region, and one who was equally fluent in both English and 'Irish' (as Scottish Gaelic was then known), he was ideally suited for the task. So he took up the challenge and started to travel widely among the islands and write his unique and memorable account of all he saw and heard. It would appear that this research was all carried out at his own expense but ultimately he was well rewarded.

It can be hard enough today to land on any island that isn't served with public transport but think how much more difficult it must have been in Martin's time! Only occasionally does he give an inkling of the problems involved. For example, at 6pm on the 29th of May, 1697 he and a new minister for the island set sail from Ensay in the Sound of Harris for St Kilda – forty miles away in the Atlantic. This was Martin's third attempt to reach the island. A favourable breeze turned against them when it was judged too late to return to Ensay so the crew rowed on a compass course for sixteen hours in atrocious weather. They made no landfall and as they saw some sea birds flying southwards they decided that they must have been blown too far north. Sure enough, after a time they spotted Boreray twelve miles to the south of them. This was 'a joyful sight, and begot new vigor in our men' who were plied 'with plenty of *aqua vitae* to support them'. They eventually reached Boreray and sheltered behind Stac an Armin as the men were utterly exhausted. But this disturbed the nesting gannets whose 'excrements were in such quantity, that they sullied our boat and cloaths'. Then a violent storm blew up which drove them out to sea again and tossed them around all night so that they 'laid aside all hopes of life'. Fortunately as the morning of 1st June dawned, 'it pleased God to command a calm day' and so they managed eventually to reach Hirta (St Kilda).

Martin spent three weeks among the islanders and contributed a paper on the subject to the Royal Society later that year which was so well received that it obviously encouraged him to continue with his research.

It is very clear from his book that he had a particular interest in medical matters and in 1710, some years after his 'best-seller' had been published in London, he chose to enter Leiden University where he studied the subject and later graduated as a doctor of medicine. However, he was already in his mid-fifties and it was obviously the academic side which had appealed to him for he never practised as a doctor. He settled in London and died, unmarried, in 1719.

There is a copy of Martin Martin's book in the National Library of Edinburgh which has been inscribed by Boswell: 'This very book accompanied Mr Samuel Johnson and me in our tour to the Hebrides in April, 1773. . . as it is the only book upon the subject, it is very well known.'

This odyssey makes no pretence to be as comprehensive as Martin Martin and certainly not as heroic as Ulysses. And although no islands produced Jason's golden fleece they all provided a wealth of golden moments in a setting every bit as colourful as Ancient Greece.

The journey starts at that famous milestone in the Firth of Clyde, Ailsa Craig, meanders among our many wonderful island archipelagoes, and finishes at that other famous milestone in the Firth of Forth – the Bass Rock.

Hamish Haswell-Smith
November 1998

Ailsa Craig

AILSA CRAIG

. . . This rock in the summer-time abounds with variety of sea-fowl, that build and hatch in it. The solan geese and coulterneb are most numerous here; the latter are by the fishers called albanich, which in the ancient Irish language signifies Scotsmen. . . .

When Ailsa Craig's ethereal shape materialises out of the mist, soaring to a height of nearly 340 metres (over 1100 feet) above the sea, one can under-stand why it was named fairy rock (*aillse creag*) by some ancient Celtic mariner. But it has also, more prosaically, been called Elizabeth's rock or Alastair's rock and its popular name nowadays is Paddy's Milestone. It is more than twelve times the area and three times the height of the Bass Rock, which is a mere pimple by comparison, and it is so precipitous that even the sea birds find it impossible to nest on some of the cliffs.

A glacier flowing down the Clyde valley 25,000 years ago, when Scotland lay smothered under a thick sheet of ice, broke off pieces of Ailsa Craig and scattered them between Wales and the Pennines in the English Midlands. They still lie there today. The rock is mainly volcanic basalt but there is a seam of reddish fine-grained micro-granite which is the ideal material for curling stones. These were quarried and cut on the island then polished on the mainland and a few are still manufactured today for connoisseurs.

It's more than a decade since I landed on Ailsa Craig. We sailed there in a trusty bilge-keeled ketch – *Jeananne* – which belonged to my present-day sailing partners. She drew only one metre which let us lie in shallow water alongside the small wooden jetty. Anchoring is not easy as the sea bottom is steep and boulder strewn.

A rusty narrow-gauge railway line runs from the jetty past the quarrymen's cottages to the old quarry on the south side. A century ago almost thirty people – quarrymen, lighthouse keepers, and their families – lived here but the quarrymen left and the lighthouse is now automatic. There are heaps of miniature Henry Moore sculptures – waste granite pieces from which the spheroidal curling stones have been cut leaving voluptuous curved forms.

A zig-zag path starts near the lighthouse and climbs past the old square keep 100 metres up the slope. It was said to be a retreat for the monks of Crossraguel Abbey (near Maybole) and that the Catholics once held it on behalf of Philip II of Spain. Further up, the path passes over the shallow valley of Garraloo and beside the tiny Garra Loch before making its way to the top. Here the world falls away in a sudden vertiginous plunge to the sea far below and the view is enthralling. Beyond the white lace of the surf lie the wide stretches of the Firth of Clyde with Arran, the Ayrshire coast, and the long dark shape of Ulster on the south-western horizon. Experienced climbers may prefer to go directly up the slope from the landing place. This is not difficult but in places the route leads over steeply inclined slabs.

Ailsa Craig is noted for its immense gannet colony which accounts for about five per cent of the world's total gannet population. There also used to be many puffins and an ornithologist reported in the 1860s that there were at least 250,000 pairs and that when he disturbed them 'their numbers seemed so great as to cause a bewildering darkness'. But in 1889 brown rats arrived off ships ferrying supplies to the newly built lighthouse and by 1984 they had wiped out the entire puffin population. (Rabbits, incidentally, were introduced about the same time by the quarrymen to supplement their diet – and were later claimed to be interbreeding with the rats!) In 1991 a massive rat eradication programme was instituted and, to date, it seems to have been successful. Puffins are, at last, visiting the island again.

Instead of climbing it is possible to complete a relatively easy two-mile circumnavigation of the island. The exposed corner at Stranny Point in the south-west is the only minor obstruction. It has to be negotiated to reach the dramatic Water Cave when coming from the east past Little Ailsa so try and time it near low water.

The names of features on Ailsa Craig are pure poetry – for example, Spot of Grass, Bare Stack, Doras Yett, Ashydoo, Rotten Nick and Kennedy's Nags. Ailsa Craig itself is mentioned in the poetry of both Wordsworth and Keats but, strangely, not by Burns who grew up within sight of it.

SANDA

. . . the isle Avon, above a mile in circumference, lies to the south of Kintyre Mull; it hath a harbour for barques on the north. . .

. . . If any man be disposed to live a solitary, retired life, and to withdraw from the noise of the world, he may have a place of retreat there in a small island, or in the corner of a large one, where he may enjoy himself, and live at a very cheap rate.

Anyone who steps on the tiny 300-acre island of Sanda which lies off the Mull of Kintyre could be seriously at risk. Legend claims that St Ninian was buried here and an ancient curse warns anyone who steps on his grave that they will die within a year. The site used to be marked by an alder tree but there are no longer any alder trees on the island and so the position of the grave is unknown.

I suppose this risk is tolerable for a short visit but it must be a continual worry for the farmer-owner, John Gannon. Whether or not he had inadvertently stepped on the grave, Mr Gannon nearly lost his life in 1996 when his boat capsized and he was trapped beneath it. Luckily there was sufficient air in the hull for him to survive until he was rescued by the Campbeltown lifeboat. Such incidents highlight the dangers of a lonely island existence and should be considered carefully by all would-be island purchasers.

Incidentally, it was the Campbeltown lifeboat which carried out the renowned rescue in 1946 of all fifty-four passengers and crew of the SS *Byron Darnton*. They were saved from the wreck in the nick of time as she broke up on the rocks on the south side of Sanda.

The Norse sometimes referred to Sanda as 'Havn' because it provided a reasonable offshore haven or harbour for boats. For many centuries this led to the island being called 'Avon' and even led to one eminent geographer wondering why an island had been given the Gaelic word for river (*abhainn*).

But if for no other reason, its anchorage makes Sanda a useful stopping-off point when waiting for a suitable tide to round the sometimes-treacherous Mull of Kintyre. It is worth going ashore on such occasions for it has the enchantment of all our islands. The farmhouse, which has been restored by the owner, is just beside the jetty and slipway and the old schoolhouse is nearby. In the 1890s this was the home of an active fishing community of thirty-six souls.

. . .a conspicious cruciform shaped stone. . .

On our last visit, *en route* for the Mull and waiting for the tide, it was Craig's unfortunate turn in the galley. Only a light lunch was required but he opted to stay aboard. We landed and followed the earth road which winds across the island from the slipway to the lighthouse. The roofless ruin of St Ninian's Chapel, pre-14th century, is beside a knoll within the burial enclosure. It has a stone basin or piscina set in the wall under one of the window embrasures and in the corner a worn Early Christian slab is incised with a cross. Near the centre of the burial ground is a conspicuous cruciform-shaped stone nearly two metres high and just west of the chapel are the footings of a small square structure. A 1630 record states: 'at the syde of that Chappell there is a litle well or compass of stones. . . And they say that the bones of certaine holie men that lived in that Illand is buried within that place.' It was a Sanda tradition that if there was a severe storm when the fishermen were still at sea the islanders would gather in the burial ground, say a prayer for them, and then solemnly pour a cup of fresh water on the ground.

Ian stayed to photograph the chapel ruins while Peter and I set off to see the lighthouse. Peter, at six foot five inches, is a useful spare mast but with his long legs he could be wearing seven-league boots. A gentle stroll can become a marathon. There was a cool wind, but the valley is sheltered and traps the sun, so our sailing jackets and jerseys were discarded by the roadside. The island had not been seriously farmed for many post-war years but now the fences had been repaired, sheep were grazing peacefully, and the owner's tractor could be heard fitfully in the distance. The lighthouse, which is on a rocky promontory on the south shore, is called 'The Ship' because, to an imaginative person on a misty day, it has that appearance. It was built in 1850. There is a huge natural stone arch beside it which frames a distant view of Ailsa Craig. There was only time for a very quick sketch before returning to *Jandara*.

When we climbed back on board, hot and thirsty, we found lunch prepared and Craig smiling happily, cool and relaxed.

'The Ship' lighthouse

The ruined chapel on Texa

TEXA

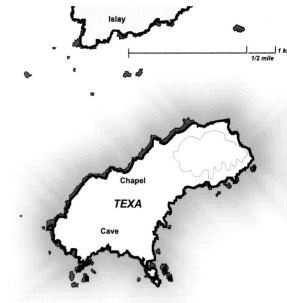

. . . There are some isles on the coast of Islay, an island Texa on the south-west, about a mile in circumference . . .

In spite of its name Texa has no connection with the Lone Star State, although I believe an American couple now own it. Abbot Adomnan of Iona referred to 'Oidecha Insula', meaning the island of (monastic) instruction, and this is said to be the derivation of its unusual name although I prefer 'Tech-oy' which means simply 'House Island' in Early Irish and Norse.

Lying off the south coast of Islay it was another of those small islands (a mere 120 acres) which was more or less on the direct route for Irish missionaries travelling to and from Scotland in the 6th century. Cainnech, or St Kenneth, was said to have left his pastoral staff behind after visiting Iona. Columba found it, blessed it, and cast it into the sea and Kenneth later discovered it washed up on the shore of Texa.

We anchored *Jandara* in the bay below the small ruined chapel. This is Lord of the Isles' territory, and just across the kyle is Lagavullin Bay and the prominent ruin of Dunyvaig Castle where the King of the Isles', Somerled's, powerful fleet used to anchor in the 12th century. The chapel was built in the late 14th century by his descendent, Ragnald, son of John of Islay, and the shaft of a cross which stood beside it was decorated with Ragnald's head. It is the earliest sculptured stone portrait of any member of the house of Somerled and it is now in the museum in Edinburgh. Round about the church bits of walling show through the turf and there are regular ridges which may well mark the remains of early monastery buildings. They indicate the position of at least five buildings. Another ruin stands some distance apart from the chapel – the abbot's house maybe? A small well to the east is dedicated to St Mary – 'Tobar Moireig'.

It is easy to imagine living a fairly comfortable monastic life on this peaceful spot. It is on record that Texa's church was endowed with large estates in the south of Islay so it was quite wealthy and the island supported about thirty native 'Texans'. It is revealing that in 1608, Andrew Knox, Bishop of the Isles, wrote a letter from Texa to King James VI asking if he could retire there – '. . . seeing my ould aige dayle crepis on'.

On our first visit – a damp day in early summer – the ground was blanketed with a mist of bluebells and feral goats watched us warily from a distance. They were in small groups but there are probably about eighty or so in total. The wild goats of Jura are a deep chocolate brown but Texa's are multi-coloured which suggests mixed domestic stock.

On the ground overlooking the kyle and some distance beyond the jetty there is a renovated cottage/bothy which the owners use occasionally. This is the only habitable building – lovely in the summer – but a lonely place to stay on a winter's night.

On the other side of Texa there is a cave called Uamh nam Fear – 'the Men's Cave' – which was probably a hideout from naval press-gangs. They particularly liked to raid islands because the able-bodied men were such excellent sailors. It was not their concern that an island needed its menfolk to survive and many of the small islands were depopulated by this practice.

On the Islay coast, Loch an t-Sàilein, reached by a circuitous route past Dunyvaig Castle and two distilleries, provides a more spacious anchorage than Lagavulin Bay. It is sheltered by a tidal island and a vast plethora of rocks. The sea barrels in between them and whips up a vicious froth – like over-boiled cullen skink. A good spot from which to visit the distilleries but not my favourite anchorage.

A sailing friend – a retired surgeon – in patched pink pants, whose 'characterful' cottage overlooks the loch, assured us that there was a short-cut through the rocks – 'Easy as pie, old boy! – Just follow the chart of '54.' His wife smiled sweetly as he kindly presented *Jandara* with a copy. It was dated '1854' and like most charts of the time was stippled with soundings like a pointillist painting. A collector's item certainly – but we didn't try the short-cut.

CARA

. . . The isle Caray. . . affords good pasturage, and abounds with coneys. There is a harbour for barks on the north-east end of it. This island is the property of MacAlister of Lergy, a family of the Macdonalds. . .

Sunlight was sparkling on the water when we sailed to Cara. Monkshaven, our anchorage opposite Cara House, is not a particularly sheltered spot but the conditions were ideal with a mere breath of breeze. The house, which was built about 1733 as a residence for the tacksman, is a dour two-storey stone building with a slated roof standing proud and lonely and staring across the Sound of Gigha towards Kintyre. It was June and the low-lying peaty ground was a sea of wildflowers as the marshy conditions here keep the bracken at bay.

Cara has only one permanent resident these days but you won't find him in any census records. 'He's a neat little man, dressed in brown, with a pointed beard,' Morton Macdonald of Largie reported to the *Observer* in 1909. He was referring to the famous Brownie of Cara who is said to be the ghost of a Macdonald murdered by a Campbell. Tradition says that he inhabits an attic room in Cara House, and that the laird and minister always raise their hats to him when they step ashore on Cara, and so should everyone else.

Some years ago, when staying (boatless) on Gigha, I was negotiating in the hotel bar with a fisherman to take Jean and me to Cara. The deal was struck but in subsequent conversation Jean happened to mention that her mother was a Campbell. 'There is no way then that I can take you to Cara,' said the fisherman. 'The Brownie would be very upset'. Persuasion was absolutely useless and the trip had to be abandoned.

On this occasion Peter and I wanted to take a close look at the 'Brownie's Chair'. We located it with some difficulty after struggling through waist-high bracken – a huge stone 'armchair', with only one arm, set on a steep slope above the sea on the east side of the the Mull of Cara. Its odd angular shape bears no relationship to the weathered rock outcrops which surround it. The 'Brownie's Well' close by is a spring which provides fresh water and has never run dry.

Cara House

Monkshaven

CARA

Brownie's Chair

1 km
1/2 mile

There are many stories telling of the Brownie's irascible disposition but impish sense of humour. I was told by an old man that on one occasion when fishing near Cara he and his son beached their boat to have a drink of water from the Brownie's Well. When they returned to the boat the thwart (benchseat) was missing. They were mystified and looked everywhere but there was no sign of it. The next day while passing the same spot they looked up and saw the thwart stuck between two rocks at the top of the hill. Obviously the Brownie had been up to his usual tricks.

There is another well east of Cara House and behind the house is a ruined chapel which can easily be mistaken for a sheep pen. It fell into disuse in the late 18th century and was used for a time as a kitchen. According to a record dated 1456 it was called 'the chapel of St Finla' and Dean Monro said it belonged to Icolmkill (Iona) and that Cara was a monks' retreat.

The island has belonged to the Macdonalds of Largie (Kintyre) for centuries. Flora MacDonald was closely related to them and some time after 1745 she and her brother stayed at Largie for a year. In the end she emigrated to Carolina after her brother was sadly killed in a shooting accident on Cara.

He may have been shooting wild goats as there are many on the island but they were concealed from us by the thick bracken which we had to plough through to reach the west side of the island. It was off here during the Second World War that a newly built P&O ship with a cargo of copra was hit by a German bomb which went straight down her funnel. The blazing hulk drifted for two days before coming to rest on Cara where she burned for a further six weeks.

For centuries Cara was the control centre for Gigha, Jura and Islay's smuggling activities. It was here in 1786 that the *Prince of Wales* revenue cutter dug up eighteen casks of foreign spirits, so it was obviously essential that the house should have a good view of the sea approach and the mainland. And I suppose it was little wonder that twinkling lights were often to be seen on dark nights in the Brownie's attic room!

The Brownie's Chair on Cara

GIGHA

There is a well in the north end of this isle called Tobermore, i.e., a great well, because of its effects, for which it is famous among the islanders; who, together with the inhabitants, use it as a catholicon for diseases. It is covered with stone and clay, because the natives fancy that the stream that flows from it might overflow the isle; and it is always opened by a diroch, i.e., an inmate, else they think it would not exert its virtues. They ascribe one very extraordinary effect to it, and it is this: that when any foreign boats are wind-bound here (which often happens) the master of the boat ordinarily gives the native that lets the water run a piece of money; and they say that immediately afterwards the wind changes in favour of those that are thus detained by contrary winds. Every stranger that goes to drink of the water of this well, is accustomed to leave on its stone-cover a piece of money, a needle, pin, or one of the prettiest variegated stones they can find.

Some of the natives told me that they used to chew nettles, and hold them to their nostrils to staunch bleeding at the nose; and that nettles being applied to the place would also stop bleeding at a vein, or otherwise.

. . . The inhabitants are all Protestants, and speak the Irish tongue generally; they are grave and reserved in their conversation; they are accustomed not to bury on Friday; they are fair or brown in complexion. . .

. . . There is only one inn. . .

I remember years ago taking the family over to Gigha in the small open ferry with a sheep for company. When we ambled along the island's main road a friendly young thrush hopped from the hedgerow onto my son's outstretched arm, and there wasn't a car in sight. Now the vehicle ferry from Tayinloan makes swift and regular crossings and fast footwork is sometimes required to avoid the island traffic.

But Gigha still retains its charm and fully justifies its Old Norse name of 'God's island' or 'the good island'. And the visiting sailor is always assured of a warm welcome – mooring buoys in Ardminish Bay, hot showers ashore and a cosy bar at the local hotel (which won an architectural award).

Gigha enjoys a key position on the sea route along the Kintyre peninsula. In the autumn of 1263 King Haakon's fleet of more than 100 ships anchored here before the Battle of

The old watermill on Gigha

Largs and was delayed by bad weather. Haakon used the time to secure the allegiance of the local chiefs and to excuse the Lord of the Isles from having to take up arms against his other overlord – the Scots' King Alexander. Another king, William of Orange, landed on Gigha in 1689 and gained the support of MacNeill of Gigha. MacNeill also remained loyal during the 1745 uprising but this is not altogether surprising as the Duke of Argyll was his overlord.

The island's renowned hospitality comes with a relaxed way of life, a nine-hole golf course, a balanced community of about 140 souls, and one of Scotland's most beautiful gardens.

When William James Yorke Scarlett, owner in the 1890s, was away on the mainland and his servants were taking time off for a round of golf, a fire burned down most of the main house. It was eventually rebuilt and renamed Achamore House. But it was Sir James Horlick (of bed-time drink fame), owner from 1944 to 1973, who converted the deciduous wood-land around it into a truly magnificent garden which he planted with many rare species collected worldwide. Apart from the varied tree cover there are rhododendron (including the famous Horlick hybrids), azalea, laburnum, *Primula candelabra*, and various sub-tropical plants such as palm lilies, palm trees and flame-trees (*Embothrium longifolium*) which grow happily in Gigha's mild climate. Sir James was a benevolent landlord who modernised the farms, built up a dairy herd, started a cheese factory, and drove through his gardens in a dragon-caparisoned motorised tricycle. He died at Achamore House in 1972. The gardens are open to the public from April to September inclusive and May is probably the best month to see them. The plants were gifted to the National Trust in 1962.

The red and yellow sandstone ruins of the 13th-century Kilchattan church are near Achamore gardens. St Catan was an Irish missionary of the 6th century who settled in Bute. There are a number of interesting carved grave-slabs in the churchyard dating back to the 14th century and the nearby ogam stone is the only example of its kind in the west of Scotland. Ogam is an ancient Celtic writing which is still largely undeciphered.

The beaches at Ardminish and the many other attractive coastal bays and inlets are of fine white Hebridean sand. There are a number of interesting caves around the coastline but the largest, Uamh Mhor on the west coast, is difficult to approach from the land. It was probably occupied in prehistoric times, was certainly a favourite hideout for smugglers, and has never been fully explored. And at the most southerly point, Sloc an Leim – 'the squirting pit' – is a long subterranean passage through which the sea rushes violently during westerly gales and then jets up to a great height like a geyser.

The two largest lochs, Mill and Upper Loch, are very ancient artificial lochs with small islets which may be crannogs. They used to be kept regularly stocked with fish, but the very narrow adjacent loch, Tarr an Tairbh ('tail of the bull'), is not recommended for fishing as it is reputed to hide a shy bull-like monster which I may have actually seen. There is a derelict watermill near Creag Bhan – Gigha's highest hill – which I wanted to sketch so Peter and I hired cycles from McSporran's Store near the ferry pier and pedalled off down the road. Rounding a bend near the Mill Loch we met an enormous bull in the middle of the track who looked decidedly unfriendly. There was no easy retreat and no time to think so we muttered a greeting and cycled past – one on each side of him. He merely snorted.

No description of Gigha should end without mention of the worthy Seumas McSporran. Apart from hiring bicycles and running a well-stocked store, he held, until his recent partial retirement, fifteen official posts including postman, policeman and registrar of births, marriages and deaths. As far as I know he has not yet conducted a church service – but give him time.

Ruins of the Augustinian Priory

ORONSAY

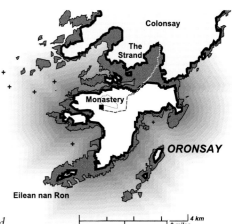

. . . The natives of Colonsay are accustomed, after their arrival in Oronsay Isle, to make a tour sunways about the church, before they enter upon any kind of business.

. . . My landlord having one of his family sick of a fever asked my book, as a singular favour, for a few moments. I was not a little surprised at the honest man's request, he being illiterate; and when he told me the reason of it I was no less amazed, for it was to fan the patient's face with the leaves of the book, and this he did at night. He sought the book next morning, and again in the evening, and then thanked me for so great a favour; and told me the sick person was much better by it. . .

Oronsay is separated from Colonsay by a wide expanse of shell sand – The Strand – which can be crossed on foot when the tide is out. If a fugitive could reach the sanctuary cross, which is halfway across, before being caught by pursuers or the tide, he was granted immunity from punishment – or so it is said.

These linked islands have been inhabited for 7000 years. Many early Christian and pre-Christian relics have been discovered including the bones of primitive domestic animals and Neolithic flint tools. The pagan ship-burial of a Viking warrior in 855 complete with his weapons, horse and coins, had been given extra insurance cover for the hereafter by the incision of two Christian crosses on stone slabs. It was uncovered in the sand dunes in 1882.

Oronsay is a tidal island, and the name normally means just that in Gaelic, but in this particular case it refers to St Oran who founded a monastery here in 563. Later, about 1380, a fine Augustinian Priory was built on the site and the ruins today run a close second to those of Iona. Some human bones from the neighbouring graveyard are kept by the high altar in the chapel and beautifully sculpted medieval tombstones are protected in a roofed building. From an architectural point of view the delightfully proportioned miniature cloisters are particularly worth seeing and in front of the group of buildings there is a remarkable 3.7 metre (12 feet) high Celtic cross on a mound. The whole island is suffused with a feeling of tranquillity and it is easy to understand why St Oran chose it for a retreat, although Columba is reputed to have rejected it because it was too near Ireland.

MacNeil of Knapdale acquired both the islands from the Campbells in 1700 and sailed over with his cattle in an open boat to take possession. MacNeil's wife is said to have given birth during the voyage and he slaughtered a cow so that mother and child could lie inside the carcass to keep warm. The MacNeils were good landlords but, unfortunately, in the manner of the time, raided the existing buildings for stone so the spacious farmhouse and outbuildings which they built next door to the Priory are part of the reason for the Priory's ruined state today. Likewise, he is thought to have completely demolished an abbey and convent in order to build Colonsay House.

This was one of the few Hebridean islands which was fortunate enough to escape the 19th-century clearances thanks to the liberal approach of John MacNeil, the laird at the time. But this was partly because so many families had already been driven by poverty to emigrate to America and the *Statistical Account* lamented, 'Pity it is that such numbers should bid farewell to their native country, when there is so great a demand for useful citizens'. By 1904 debt had forced the MacNeils to put the island up for sale and it was bought by Lord Strathcona in 1905. The Strathcona family still own Colonsay but sold Oronsay in the 1970s.

A reef of islets and some skerries lie parallel to the east coast of Oronsay, creating a channel, Caolas Mór, which is the only partially sheltered anchorage in the area. There are a number of Mesolithic shell mounds near the shore as it was the site of a Stone Age settlement. A small sandy beach and boat house face the kyle and it was here we anchored *Jandara*. Unfortunately there are no secure anchorages round Colonsay or Oronsay and we've spent uncomfortable nights on several different occasions off the ferry pier at Scalasaig.

Oronsay's American owner runs a trim farm on the island and it is pleasant to see well-repaired dykes and fences. The flat area to the south is used as an airstrip but landing must be hazardous as ponies wander across it and thousands of excavating rabbits are hard at work. Beyond the airstrip is a long reef ending with the ruin of an old kelp-gatherer's cottage on Eilean nan Ron – 'seal island' – which is well-named and a nature reserve. A thousand or more grey Atlantic seals converge here every autumn and the roar of battling bulls can be heard for miles.

EILEACH AN NAOIMH

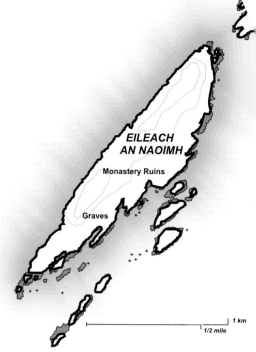

. . . In the ninth year of Meilochen, son to Pridius, King of Picts, a most powerful king, Columbus, by his preaching and example, converted that nation to the faith of Christ. Upon this account, they gave him Iona to erect a monastery in. . . and where he was buried in the 77th year of his age. . .

He built a noble monastery in Ireland before his coming to Britain, from both which monasteries he and his disciples founded several other monasteries in Britain and Ireland, among all which the monastery of the island in which his body is interred has the pre-eminence. . .

If the madding crowd of tourists on Iona get you down then why not escape, like St Columba, to his private island paradise? He would slip away for a rest cure on tranquil Eileach an Naoimh, the southernmost of the chain of small islands known today as the Garvellachs. It was here that his uncle, St Brendan of Clonfert, had founded a small rural monastery in AD542 – twenty-one years before Columba himself founded Iona – and it offered him a blessed place of peace.

Eileach an Naoimh is early Gaelic for the 'rocky place of the saint' and when Adomnan, Abbot of Iona, wrote about his predecessor he mentioned Columba's great love of 'Hinba' – the 'Isles of the Sea'. It is almost certain that this refers to the Garvellachs. The early Celtic monks tried to emulate the devotion of St John the Baptist by looking for spiritual uplift in the wilderness, and what better place in the Scottish context than a small island in the ocean wastes?

But although this island is a 'rocky place' much of the rock is limestone, so the soil is fertile and the grass green. As the strata tilt upwards, ending in steep cliffs, the south-facing slopes and rocky crevices are sheltered from the prevailing winds and covered with a riot of scarlet pimpernel, primrose, yellow iris, meadow-sweet and honeysuckle. A splendid natural sandstone arch, An Chlàrsach – 'the harp', at the north end of the island can be reached by an interesting but rough walk along the shore, or on the springy turf along the top of the ridge with the sea frothing at the foot of the cliffs below you.

The anchorage is in a lagoon formed by a line of skerries where a tiny creek with a shingle beach is called the 'port for Columba's church'. Beside it a fresh-water spring runs into a stone basin overgrown with watercress and beyond can be seen the low broken ruin

19

of the monastery and a church with a chancel and mortared walls. These are thought to date from the 9th century (St Brendan's original structures would almost certainly have been of wood) but the settlement was destroyed in the 10th century, probably by Norsemen. Just north is a small cell and beyond it a chapel with walls nearly one metre thick and an indecipherable carved slab inside. There is open space around the chapel with a low vallum or rampart at the foot of the hillside and, further to the north, the remains of a stone kiln in which the monks baked bread, or maybe dried corn, and a structure that may have been a winnowing barn.

A natural rock 'pulpit' stands by the landing place near the shore and on the slope above it there are two partly reconstructed semi-detached beehive cells – the finest examples of these ancient structures in all Scotland. One of the cells of this *clochain* – as the double cell is called – could have been an oratory with an underground cell beside it, like a Pictish souterrain, which may have been a wine cellar.

There is also a burial ground with a number of upended slabs. Many carved tombs, ornamented stones and crosses were reported in 1824, when the ruins were 'discovered', but through the years these have been stolen.

Columba's mother, Eithne, Princess of Leinster, is supposed to be buried here and a small upright slate slab roughly incised with a cross marks the spot. His uncle, Brendan, is said to be buried on the next-door islet, A' Chuli. St Columba's remains were moved from Iona to an unknown destination in the 9th century during the Norse raids and his grave has never been located. Is it possible that he had originally asked to be buried on his beloved Eileach an Naoimh and that the monks belatedly carried out his wish?

Beehive cells on Eileach an Naoimh

In the Corryvreckan

SCARBA

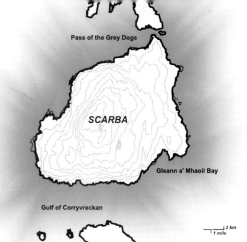

. . . the famous and dangerous gulf, called Cory Vrekan. . . yields an impetuous current, not to be matched anywhere about the isle of Britain. The sea begins to boil and ferment with the tide of flood, and resembles the boiling of a pot; and then increases gradually, until it appears in many whirlpools, which form themselves in sort of pyramids, and immediately after spout up as high as the mast of a little vessel, and at the same time make a loud report. These white waves run two leagues with the wind before they break. . . This boiling of the sea is not above a pistol-shot distant from the coast of Scarba Isle, where the white waves meet and spout up: they call it the Kaillach, i.e., an old hag; and they say that when she puts on her kerchief, i.e., the whitest waves, it is then reckoned fatal to approach her. . .

Once upon a time a handsome young prince sailed over from Scandinavia and fell in love with the beautiful daughter of a Jura chieftain. He asked for her hand in marriage, but her father had other plans. 'No problem.' he said. 'Take your boat and anchor it for three consecutive days in the middle of the Gulf between Jura and Scarba and then you can marry my daughter.'

Prince Breacan agreed but he smelt a rat and asked the local sailors for their advice. The waters are dangerous and there is only one way to survive, they told him. You must use three ropes for your anchor, one made of wool, one of hemp, and one of virgins' hair. So the prince travelled round Jura and Scarba collecting the materials and at last the ropes were made to his satisfaction. He then sailed his boat out to the middle of the Gulf and dropped anchor.

At the end of the first day the wool rope parted, and by the end of the second day the hemp rope had broken. Then on the third day it became clear that the island girls had not been entirely honest because the hair rope also broke and the prince was drowned. And the chieftain's daughter lived unhappily ever after and the Gulf became known as the Corryvreckan (Breacan's cauldron).

This sad little story is, of course, entirely untrue.

The flood tides from the Irish Sea run up the Sound of Jura building up a huge head of water which forces itself westwards out through the Gulf of Coire Bhreacain ('the speckled cauldron') and runs headlong into the incoming Atlantic tide. Down below this thundering collision, the bottom of the gulf has been shaped by a primeval cataclysm. A ridge runs out from Scarba with a high rock pinnacle on the end of it and in the centre of the gulf a narrow pit, like a gateway to hell, descends 100 metres below the surrounding seabed to an overall depth of 219 metres. The turbulent waters spin round the pinnacle creating a maelstrom. In westerly gales there are also enormous breakers, violent eddies and water spouts and the noise of these overfalls can be heard many miles away. It is one of Europe's most dramatic seascapes and even at slack water, when it is possible to sail through the Gulf, the turgid eddies and whorls sucking at the surface create a palpable sense of menace.

Scarba itself is a rugged island, a single peak rising to a height of 449 metres above sea-level with many coastal cliffs and caves and set between two notorious tidal races – the Corryvreckan to the south and the Pass of the Grey Dogs to the north. The west flank is the most precipitous but the east side is gentler, with a small patch of land fit for cultivation, and some scattered woodland. This 3600-acre island once supported fourteen families but nowadays it has no permanent residents and belongs to the family of the late Lord Duncan Sandys.

Gleann a' Mhaoil Bay – just round the corner from the Corryvreckan – has a beach of large, multi-coloured pebbles and a small cottage which is occupied in summer by the wardens of an adventure school. They train school children in survival techniques – how to live entirely off the land and use the caves for shelter. There is an interesting trudge up the ridge beside this bothy which Peter and I tried out a couple of years ago. . . up and over the ridge. . . and the next ridge. . . and the next again. The going was rough: tufts of ankle-twisting grass, heather, and bracken with boggy patches amid great swathes of ragged-robin and cotton grass. Behind the ridges a vestigial path ran alongside a small loch. Only a narrow earth barrier seemed to stop this lochan from emptying itself nearly 300 metres down the mountain-side. Following the 'path' round the contours until it disappeared brought us to the head of a steep gully which falls dramatically down to Camas nam Bàirneach ('limpet creek'). Deer spied on us from every rocky outcrop and far below the largest of the Corryvreckan whirlpools was taking shape in a white froth. A thrilling viewpoint!

EILEAN RIGH

. . . The manner of drinking used by the chief men of the isles is called. . . a 'round'; for the company sat in a circle, the cup-bearer filled the drink round to them, and all was drunk out whatever the liqour was, whether strong or weak; they continued drinking sometimes twenty-four, sometimes forty-eight hours. It was reckoned a piece of manhood to drink until they became drunk, and there were two men with a barrow attending punctually on such occasions. They stood at the door until some became drunk, and they carried them upon the barrow to bed. . .

. . . Among persons of distinction it was reckoned an affront put upon any company to broach a piece of wine, ale, or aquavitae and not to see it all drunk out at one meeting.

No one can be sure how Eilean Righ – the 'Royal Island' – got its name. It may have been named after the Danish sea-king Olaf who is reputed to have died in this region or it might have been in honour of one of the many early Scottish kings who were crowned in mid-Argyll, but whatever its true history it is easy to see it as a modest place of royal residence. It had, in any case, a more recent royal association for it belonged to Sir Reginald Fleming Johnston, the famous tutor of Pu Yi, the last emperor of China. In the film *The Last Emperor*, Johnston was portrayed by Peter O'Toole. In 1934, after he had retired from his work in China and returned to Scotland with his Chinese mistress, Sir Reginald modernised the island's two houses and settled in with his memories. It was here that he wrote the greater part of his book *Twilight in the Forbidden City*.

Eilean Righ (pron. *elan ree*), not much more than a mere 200 acres in area, is snugly situated in Loch Craignish, a sea-loch which is separated from the Sound of Jura by the powerful tidal rips of the Dorus Mór. A little further south is Crinan and the entrance to the canal which links to Loch Fyne. With good hill pasture and a fairly large area of mature woodland consisting of oak, ash, rowan, alder and hawthorn spreading along its east shore, the island was bought in 1992 by Viscount Chewton (a Somerset farmer and brother of the former government minister, William Waldegrave). He had spent all his childhood holidays on Scottish islands and he wanted his sons to have the same wonderful experience. But for family reasons he put the island back on the market a few years later and Eilean Righ now has another owner.

The road from the newly constructed jetty climbs steeply through the dense belt of mixed woodland, stippled with primroses amid a tangle of brambles, before it reaches the attractive group of buildings. These are almost at the centre of the island and they are set round a courtyard with a central flagpole. There is also the remains of a Confucian temple and stone lantern built by Sir Reginald who owned many Chinese artefacts and antiques. When he died, there was a local report that valuable porcelain and china were thrown into the loch, but this seems a very unlikely story.

Wandering about the island in the summer months is difficult because the dense, uncontrolled growth of bracken has taken over much of the grazing land but it is worthwhile battling through it to see one of Eilean Righ's two Iron Age duns or forts which is set on the grassy summit of a ridge to the north of the buildings. It is oval-shaped and a number of minor artefacts were recovered from it by archaeologists during excavations in 1982. The other dun – Dun Righ, on a flat-topped ridge in the south-west, is rectangular but has an oval structure in the corner and just south of it is a fine example of a large cup-mark on a lichen-covered rock. This surely must have been a very important island to have justified having two forts!

The trees attract a lot of birds. Raptors and owls can be seen, and even the occasional pheasant pays a visit from the mainland. From October to March wintering divers frequent the shores which also support extensive wild mussel beds. There is a small resident herd of wild goats on Eilean Righ, although I have not yet seen them, and one would assume that they might occasionally swim over to the nearby islet which is called Eilean nan Gabhar – 'isle of the goats' – but I must admit that I have never yet seen any goats on it either. This tiny islet is probably better known for the shelter it gives to the occasional boat which tucks into the pleasant anchorage between it and the reef.

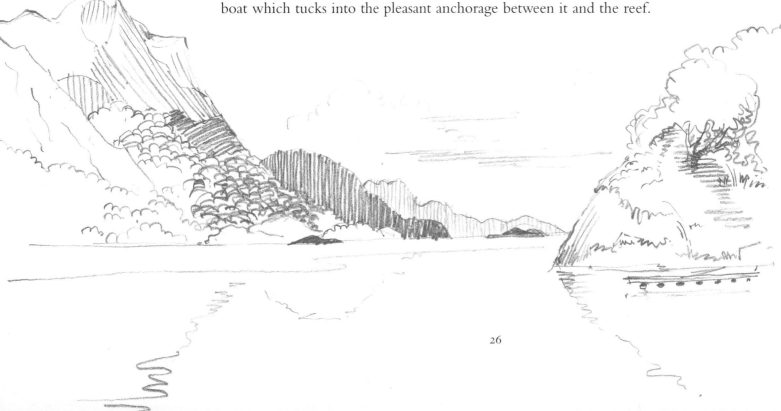

On Eilean Righ

Irene's house at Ardinamir

LUING

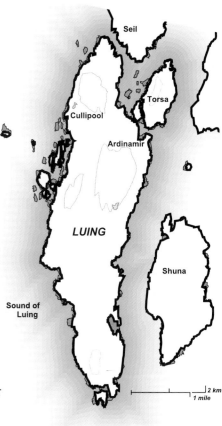

. . . Children, horses, and cows see the second sight, as well as men and women advanced in years.

There is a popular anchorage at Ardinamir on Luing and the track leading to it passes a patch of woodland and a small house with an Iron Age fort on the hill above. On summer nights pipistrelle bats catch midges among the trees. The small house was occupied by Irene – a noteworthy character (every inhabited island has at least one noteworthy character). She had no electricity supply and had rejected the Council's offer to arrange a connection on the grounds that electricity was of no use for anything – 'except for the television – and who would want the television?' she would shout (Irene assumed everyone was deaf). We never dared to ask her about the plumbing. An outside stand-pipe was her only source of running water and – to our continual puzzlement – she appeared to have no toilet facilities whatsoever, although she did have a telephone.

Because she always took such an interest in the anchorage at Ardinamir – she painted a white leading mark on a rock to help entering yachts, collected rainfall statistics, and had kept a register of all visiting yachts since the 1940s – Irene was made an honorary member of the Clyde Cruising Club. The entrance to the anchorage is through a very narrow and shallow gap between submerged reefs, tricky at the best of times, but if any helmsman was ever foolish enough to graze a rock Irene's stentorian advice could be heard on the mainland; a sound that could strike terror into any sailor's heart.

Irene spent most of her time on the bench seat at the open window admiring the West Coast Drizzle and watching the yachts entering and leaving Ardinamir. She prided herself on remembering the names of every visitor but, sadly, the passing years brought uncertainty. The one and only armchair was the property of McElvie, a very large cat with pink eyes.

We were signing the register one day and McElvie, for once, was not occupying his armchair. Irene was at the open window, dressed as usual in woolly jersey and jeans, when a couple appeared with a large black Labrador. They entered the room to greet her and were immediately asked where the dog was.

'He's waiting outside,' they said.

'Quickly!' Irene bellowed, 'You must get to him before McElvie does!'

On another occasion, since we were in the vicinity, we decided to anchor for the night at Ardinamir. It was Peter's turn to prepare the evening meal and Craig was absorbed in his favourite occupation, crouching in the lazarette (the warmest place aboard) tuning the diesel-fired heating system – which occasionally worked. Ian and I went ashore to see Irene. She welcomed us from the open window. McElvie was asleep in his armchair.

'Thank you for your postcard,' shouted Irene to Ian as soon as we had entered ' – and that will do for a Christmas Card too, mind.'

We discussed sailing, local topics, signed the register, and shared some shortbread which we had brought along. The telephone rang from beneath a heap of old newspapers on the stone floor.

'Och, that terrible machine,' yelled Irene, 'and it will not be for me at all. It is for you, of course,' she said to Ian and sat back.

McElvie's red eyes were open and staring malevolently at him. Ian rummaged under the newspapers, picked up the telephone and put it uncertainly to his ear. To his surprise it was his wife, Jean, trying to contact him urgently, and she had only tried telephoning Irene on the wildest improbability.

McElvie's eyes panned slowly round and met mine. Then they closed and dismissed us all.

All things change. Irene, sadly, is no longer with us, after a spell in Oban (where she enjoyed watching television). McElvie, a pathetic shadow of his former self, and semi-wild, would come out of the shrubs to greet us for a while, but now, like Irene, he too has faded away.

Luing, which has one of the largest lobster-ponds in Scotland and its own famous and unique breed of prize beef cattle, is an easy island to reach from the mainland as there is a fast and regular car-ferry service across the 200 metres wide Cuan Sound which separates it from the island of Seil. Seil in turn is linked to the mainland by the famous 'Bridge over the Atlantic'. From the attractive village of Toberonochy in the south to the equally delightful village of Cullipool in the north, Luing has the gentle country atmosphere of a much more mellow age – except for the northern corner which is a dramatic contrast.

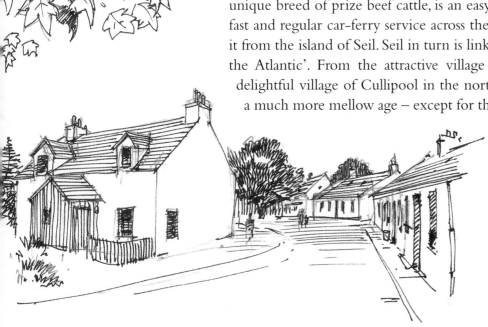

Slate used to be the principal industry (Iona Cathedral is roofed with Luing slates) but the quarry was abandoned in 1965 and it stands there now in deserted glory, a gargantuan composition of steel-grey slabs and platters, reminiscent of a Paolozzi sculpture.

KERRERA

. . . the bays afford all sorts of shellfish in great plenty; as oysters, clams, mussels, lobsters, cockles, etc., which might be pickled and exported in great quantities.

Some years ago we moored *Jandara* in Ardantrive Bay at the north end of the pleasantly rural island of Kerrera. Kerrera, which forms a natural breakwater for the important harbour of Oban, once had a population of nearly 200 and still supports about forty residents. The island's main function for many years was a stepping-stone for the annual cattle drive from Mull to the mainland.

It was a damp evening and Peter, Ian and I retired below to find the saloon chilly and unwelcoming. Craig, who is our expert on such matters, disappeared into the lazaret and twenty minutes later warm air was circulating pleasantly. He had fitted a larger diesel jet in the heating system, he explained.

Some time later, food, sea air, warmth and wine were having their inevitable effect. The ship-to-shore radio spluttered occasionally in the background. Someone was calling Oban Coastguard about a yacht which was on fire and there appeared to be no one aboard.

'Where are you?' asked the Coastguard.

'Ardantrive,' said the caller.

We grabbed our cameras and rushed on deck. Our motivation may have been heroic dreams of rescue or a photographic scoop – but more likely it was pure mindless curiosity.

We peered through a dense cloud of black exhaust fumes coming from our heating system and with great difficulty saw the red-faced skipper of the adjoining craft asking the Coastguard to cancel the call as it now appeared that there were four men aboard the yacht and that they had the emergency under control.

We switched off the heating system, thanked both the helpful caller and the Coastguard for their concern, and retired shame-facedly to our bunks.

Most of Kerrera's 3000 acres have belonged to the Clan MacDougall since Somerled's time in the 12th century. Although it is so close to bustling Oban it is a world apart with lovely views and quiet walks. An easy climb up Càrn Breugach through shrub woodland is rewarding for its magnificent view of the Lorn coast.

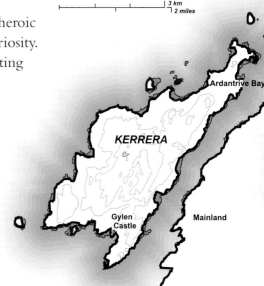

AN ISLAND
ODYSSEY

———

Kerrera

It was in Horseshoe Bay in the beautiful Sound of Kerrera that Alexander II's fleet anchored in July 1249. Alexander slept aboard ship. In the morning he said he had dreamed that St Columba had come aboard and told him he should return home immediately. Alexander's nobles felt he should heed the warning but Alexander scoffed at the idea and went ashore. But as he stepped off the vessel onto Kerrera's soil he stumbled and before he could be carried back on board he died. The land behind the bay is still called Dalrigh – 'the field of the king'.

The tall ruin of Gylen Castle – 'castle of the springs' – is on the south coast of Kerrera above natural springs which provided ample fresh water in case of siege. It was built in 1587 by the 16th MacDougall chief, on the site of an earlier fortification. In 1647 during the Covenanting Wars it was besieged by General Leslie who promised the defenders safe passage if they surrendered. They accepted, but as soon as they had left the castle every single one of them was slaughtered and the castle burnt. On a gloomy day the ruin still looks formidable poised above the steep and rocky coastline and an inscription inside seems to say – 'Trust in God and sin no more'.

Gylen Castle was the repository for the MacDougalls' famous Brooch of Lorn which is said to have belonged to Bruce. It is a large disc of Celtic silver filagree with a cavity for sacred relics and a huge rock-crystal circled by eight jewelled obelisks. For two centuries the MacDougalls believed that it had been destroyed in the fire but in 1825 General Sir Duncan Campbell of Lochnell confessed to having inherited it. His ancestor, Campbell of Inverawe, one of Leslie's officers, had looted it after all the defenders had been massacred and before the castle was burnt down. The General chose to make amends by presenting it to his neighbour, MacDougall of Dunollie, at a public ceremony.

Opposite: Gylen Castle

Achadun Castle

LISMORE

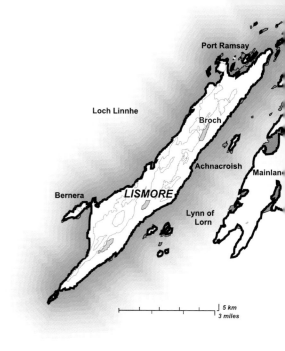

. . . It is not the habit that makes the monk, nor doth the garb in fashion qualify him that wears it to be virtuous. The inhabitants have humanity, and use strangers hospitably and charitably.

Howling wind, driving rain and failing light are not the best conditions for trying a new passage between strange rocks and I was unwise to consider it but we were all tired and with one of the crew very seasick I thought the short-cut would be worthwhile. I knew the north passage into Port Ramsay at Lismore like the back of my hand but the sailing instructions made the west passage between two skerries seem easy – and it would save nearly half an hour of further misery. 'The face of the southerly pair of cottages (and only these) kept in sight leads clear north of the rock. . . ' said the instructions. Harry had the binoculars and Duncan was at the bow as I brought *Jandara* round and headed for the distant cottages which could be seen faintly through the spume. Suddenly we came to a shuddering stop and there was a crash from below as we reared gently upwards and then slipped back again. Fortunately our speed had been slow, the rock well-cushioned with seaweed and the crash was our seasick sailor falling down the companionway with, luckily, no serious consequences except injured pride. I bore away hastily and resigned myself to a slow slog against the wind.

By comparison the Lynn of Lorn is relatively free of rocks and the story goes that in AD561 two competitive saints, St Moluag and St Mulhac, had a boat race across it after agreeing that the first to touch Lismore would be entitled to found his monastery on the island. St Moluag realised at the last minute that he would not reach the island first so he cut off his finger and threw it ashore. It landed on the beach just north of the broch at Tirefour and this gained him the title.

St Moluag was an Irish contemporary of St Columba and his monastery became an important ecclesiastical centre. More than six centuries later when John the Englishman, Bishop of Dunkeld and Argyll, confessed to the Pope that he was unable to learn to speak Gaelic, the Pope split the diocese and Lismore was chosen as the seat of a separate diocese of Argyll whose bishops were known as *Episcopi Lismorenses*.

Lismore soil is exceptionally fertile thanks to its limestone base and this probably accounts for its name – lios-mór in Gaelic which means 'big garden'. The wild flowers are profuse – field gentians, rock rose, mimulus, tutsan, ivy-leaved toadflax, wild orchids, cranesbill, brooklimes, water mints and speedwells to name a few. There are many fine trees and shelter belts, mainly sycamore, ash, lime and chestnut, but little natural woodland, although in the 16th century the whole island was very thickly forested with oak.

There is a limestone quarry at An Sàilein ('the creek'), with ivy-covered kilns and roofless cottages, which was abandoned during World War II. Carthorses from far afield were once landed at the quarries' old quay as Lismore men were noted for their ability to break them in. The lime was shipped from Port Ramsay in the north – a bay overlooked by a neat row of limeburners' cottages, most of which are now holiday homes. Apart from being a popular anchorage for yachts this anchorage is now used as an overnight stop by the occasional workboat from the giant quarry at Glensanda on the Morvern coast.

The main road runs down the spine of Lismore, which now has a population of only 140, through scattered crofts and farms. The ruin of a galleried broch known as Tirefour Castle is prominent on the summit of a high grassy knoll close to the east coast. Almost opposite it, on the west coast, Coeffin Castle, a ruined 13th-century structure, was probably built by the MacDougalls of Lorn on the site of a Viking fortress. The car-ferry pier is at Achnacroish where there is a general store and a junior school. Two ferries serve the island, a passenger ferry from Port Appin, and a car ferry from Oban.

Bernera on the west coast is more of a peninsula than an island and was once known as 'Berneray of the Noble Yew', a tree under which St Columba was said to have preached. The ancient yew was felled in 1850 to make a staircase in Lochnell Castle on the mainland and the remains of the small island chapel have disappeared. The noble ruin of Achadun Castle – the Bishop's castle – overlooks Bernera although this was some distance from the small cathedral which was founded at the start of the 13th century at Kilmoluaig (St Moluag's cell or church). The cathedral was burnt during the Reformation but in 1749 the remaining walls of the choir were reduced in height and roofed to create the present tiny parish church. There are some fine medieval tombstones in the graveyard which is also reputed to be St Moluag's burial site.

For delightful walking country Lismore is supreme – a long narrow island of nearly 6000 acres with an undulating landscape of shallow longitudinal valleys. The walk along the ridge must be one of the finest walks in Scotland, with views which are unequalled anywhere.

ULVA

. . . Near to the north-east end of Mull. . . is a capacious and excellent bay, called Toubir Mory. . .

. . . One of the ships of the Spanish Armada perished in this bay in the year 1588. There was a great sum of gold and money on board the ship, which disposed the Earl of Argyll, and some Englishmen, to attempt the recovery of it; but how far the latter succeeded in this enterprise is not generally well known. . . Several of the inhabitants of Mull told me that they had conversed with their relations that were living at the harbour when this ship was blown up; and they gave an account of an admirable providence that appeared in the preservation of one Doctor Beaton (the famous physician of Mull), who was on board the ship when she blew up, and was then sitting on the upper deck, which was blown up entire, and thrown a good way off; yet the doctor was saved; and lived several years after.

. . . Upon the north side of Loch-Scafford lies the isle of Ulva; it is three miles in circumference, and encompassed with rocks and shelves, but fruitful in corn, grass, &c.

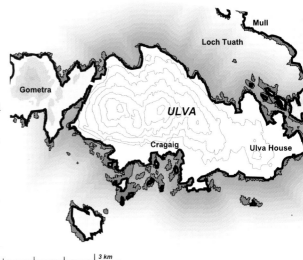

Ulva – 'Wolf Island' – is just a stone's throw from Mull. Traditionally a hail from Mull calls the ferry over but when the wind blows it is not always so easy to attract the ferryman's attention and this narrow stretch of water can be whipped up into quite a frenzy when the wind decides to show its real strength.

In his famous poem Thomas Campbell told the sad story of the Chief of Ulva eloping with Lord Ullin's daughter during a violent storm and pleading desperately: 'Boatman, do not tarry! And I'll give thee a silver pound to row us o'er the ferry.' As the enraged Lord Ullin was hard on the couple's heels the gallant ferryman agreed but her father arrived some moments later to find that: ''Twas vain: the loud waves lashed the shore, return or aid preventing; The waters wild went o'er his child, and he was left lamenting.' The lovers are reputed to be buried on the Mull shore in a grave between Oskamull Farm and Ulva Ferry.

In October 1773, some years before Campbell's poem was published, Dr Johnson and James Boswell were invited to visit Ulva by MacQuarrie, the Laird. In Boswell's own words:

'. . .a servant was sent forward to the ferry, to secure the boat for us: but the boat was gone to the Ulva side, and the wind was so high that the people could not hear him call;

and the night so dark that they could not see a signal. We should have been in a very bad situation, had there not fortunately been lying in the little sound of Ulva an Irish vessel. . . (which) ferried us over.

'M'Quarrie's house was mean; but we were agreeably surprised with the appearance of the master whom we found to be intelligent, polite and much a man of the world. Though his clan is not numerous, he is a very ancient Chief. . . He told us his family had possessed Ulva for 900 years; but I was distressed to hear that it was soon to be sold for payment of his debts.'

And it was eventually sold, yet while the MacQuarries were still the owners it was recorded that every family on the island owned at least one boat and that there were surplus crops of potatoes for export – so the 800 islanders at least enjoyed a reasonable standard of living.

The MacQuarries were Clan Chiefs of the old school, patriarchal and benevolent. To prove it Boswell reported that MacQuarrie had the right to have 'the first night of all his vassal's wives' but that he always accepted a sheep instead! Boswell added, rather wistfully, 'I suppose Ulva is the only place where this custom remains'.

The good times came to an end in 1845 when Ulva was purchased by the notorious Mr FW Clark. In just four years he ruthlessly deported over two-thirds of the total population. There is a delightful anchorage on the south side of Ulva close to the ruined watermill of Cragaig – a lovely spot – yet among the many old blackhouse ruins to be seen around it there are some with lintels still over their doors as though the evictions had taken place quite recently.

The MacQuarrie's 'mean' house was later rebuilt by the new owner to an Adam design and it was visited and praised by Sir Walter Scott. Unfortunately it was destroyed by fire but the present Ulva House stands in pleasant woodland on the same site. Virtually all the occupied dwellings on Ulva, and a small chapel, are grouped at the east end of the island in the neighbourhood of the ferry.

Ulva is full of interest. It has been designated an Area of Outstanding Natural Beauty with its many beautiful walks and nature trails and its central mountain ridge. There are hares, otters and red deer along with an enormous variety of birdlife that even includes the elusive corncrake.

The 'father of Australia', General Lachlan MacQuarie (1761-1824), was born on Ulva. He instituted liberal penal reforms in Australia while serving as governor of New South Wales but this made him so unpopular with the settlers that he had to be recalled.

Ulva's 6000 acres are owned today by the Howards and managed by their ex-Army son, Jamie. They have an oyster farm and run The Boathouse, a restaurant serving delicious fresh oysters and Guinness. Visitors are always welcome: just hail Donald Munro, the ferryman – and he won't demand a 'silver pound'.

Fingal's Cave

STAFFA

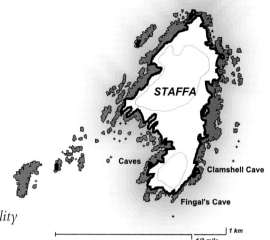

. . . The modern itch after the knowledge of foreign places is so prevalent that the generality of mankind bestow little thought or time upon the place of their nativity. It is become necessary in those of quality to travel young into foreign countries, whilst they are absolute strangers at home; and many of them when they return are only loaded with superficial knowledge. . . late fashions, new dishes, new tunes, new dances, and the like.

After Sir Joseph Banks had returned from Captain Cook's famous first voyage to Australia, and become President of the Royal Society, he set off in August 1772 to undertake botanical research in Iceland. Due to bad weather his ship took refuge in the Sound of Mull and there a Mr Leach told him about an extraordinary little island which he was sure would interest him. Banks immediately made arrangements to visit it. When he landed on Staffa he opted to spend the night in the 'house' of the island's sole inhabitants while his friends wisely stayed in a tent and as a result he was very badly infested with lice. Nevertheless Banks waxed lyrical about Staffa and following his report when back in London, tourists began to appear in droves. Among them in subsequent years were Sir Walter Scott, Keats, Mendelssohn, Turner, Wordsworth, Queen Victoria and Prince Albert, Jules Verne, Dr David Livingstone and Robert Louis Stevenson.

Fionn MacCool, the legendary Irish hero who was known to the Scots as Fingal (*fionn na ghal* – 'chief of valour'), is said to have defended the Hebrides against early raids by the Vikings and to have died in battle in Ulster in 283. His name was given to the cave by Sir Joseph Banks because, as someone explained twelve years later, the local name for the cave was An Uamh Bhinn ('the melodious cave') and his interpreter mistook this for the Gaelic genetive form of Fingal – *Finn*. I would have thought a more likely possibility is that either Banks or the interpreter heard a word like 'Fingal' being pronounced and assumed it referred to the Irish hero (the Gaelic term for a Norseman who had settled in the Hebrides is *Fionnghall* – meaning a fair-haired stranger). Most Gaelic place names tend to be practical rather than poetic, so it is possible that the cave was simply known locally as the Norseman's cave. The Norse named the island Staffa because its basalt columns resembled the vertical log staves used by them for house construction.

The regularity of these dark fine-grained basalt columns, regular haxagons or pentagons, is so perfect that it is sometimes difficult to believe that they are natural formations. They are a result of the same slow-cooling volcanic activity which created the Giant's Causeway in Ulster.

Staffa is not an easy island to visit because it is only possible to land when the sea is calm. This was possibly the reason why Boswell and Johnson failed to to mention Fingal's cave although they were in the vicinity only one year after Sir Joseph Banks had 'discovered' it. When we anchored off Staffa we were very fortunate because the conditions were perfect. It was very early on a beautiful May morning, the sea lay like molten lead, it was warm in the sun, and we had the island to ourselves. The sculptured forms, sharply etched in the clear morning light, had a surreal quality. The landing place is beside Am Buachaille, a dramatic tidal islet composed of gracefully bent columns in a curious pyramid shape. Nearby, across a narrow channel, Clamshell Cave has an entrance portico of gracefully twisted columns resembling a giant scallop. Shags gave eerie warnings from their nests in the shadows.

A path across the natural hexagonal paving leads along the colonnaded cliff-face and round the corner to Fingal's Cave which is spectacular and quite unique. It is lined with glossy hexagonal columns which on the west side rise symmetrically out of the sea. The roof, like a complicated Gothic vault, is twenty metres (65 feet) high. A rough path runs among stumps of column to the back of the cave and below it is a twenty-metre deep arm of seawater which sighs with the swell. It is navigable by dinghy.

Mendelssohn visited the island in 1829 and was inspired by it to write his Hebrides Overture (*Die Fingalshöhle*). Crowds can destroy the magic so it is best to visit the island in May or June. Wordsworth was disgusted at being accompanied by too large a crowd of fellow travellers in 1833:

> We saw, but surely in the motley crowd
> Not one of us has felt, the far-famed sight;
> How could we feel it? Each the others blight,
> Hurried and hurrying volatile and loud.

Round the southern end of the island and west of Fingal's Cave is the Colonnade, a vast expanse of columns reaching seventeen metres towards the sky with Boat Cave below them. Further round on the west side Mackinnon's Cave (named after Abbot MacKinnon of Iona who died in 1500) is almost as grand as Fingal's and has a tunnel connection through to Cormorant Cave.

Staffa is, justly, world-renowned and on Lake Zurich in Switzerland the town of Stäfa was named in honour of this little island, long ago, by a monk from Iona.

LUNGA

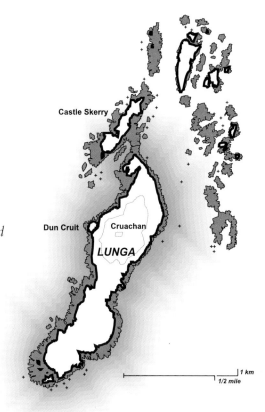

. . . the small isles called Kernburg-More and Kernburg-Beg. . . are naturally very strong, faced all round with a rock, having a narrow entry, and a violent current of a tide on each side, so that they are almost impregnable. A very few men are able to defend these two forts against a thousand. There is a small garrison of the standing forces in them at present.

. . . To the south of these forts lie the small isles of Fladday, Lungay, Back, and the Call of the Back; cod and ling are to be had plentifully about all these islands. . .

The puffin studied me quizzically as I sat in the grass with my sketchbook and then stepped solemnly towards me. He took up a position about a yard away, cocked his head on one side, put his hands behind his back, and gave me a look which said, 'OK. Sketch me now.'

I was on Lunga in the Treshnish Isles and these comic little birds were all around me. One stood on a rock like a preacher with his congregation, another strutted slowly around deep in thought, examining the ground, and several pairs whispered confidentially to each other. Occasionally one would suddenly remember he had a family to support – nod to his friends and, looking very important, run off the clifftop and spreadeagle himself on the wind, fat little body hanging there, spindly legs and big feet.

Lunga is a wonderland for birdwatchers and the occasional boatload of sightseers from Fionnphort or Dervaig on Mull stop here after a visit to Fingal's Cave. At 200 acres it is the largest of the Treshnish Isles – although Bac Mór, that ancient volcano with a lava platform brim which is better known as the Dutchman's Cap, is much more prominent from a distance. And historically its northern neighbours with their ruined forts, Cairn na Burgh More and Cairn na Burgh Beg, are much more important. The Lord of the Isles acquired the Treshnish in 1354 because they held a key frontier position between the Nordreys and Sudreys – the Northern and Southern Isles of the Norsemen. More recently, they were bought (in 1938) by the explorer and naturalist Colonel Niall Rankin and we have him to thank for carefully maintaining them as a nature reserve. Lunga is now a designated Site of Special Scientific Interest.

The Old Norse name for this narrow volcanic slab with a flat top and a single peak means 'an island shaped like a longship' or, just, 'longship-island'. Lunga's only other conspicuous feature, besides the 100-metre high Cruachan, is Dun Cruit, or Harp Rock, a sharply angled promontory, almost a stack, with a deep, narrow chasm beside it into which the sea surges noisily. The shape is reminiscent of Boreray in the St Kilda group although the comparative scale is tiny. The grassy summit, and the edge of the surrounding cliffs are pitted with puffin burrows and the cliff ledges and rocky foreshore provide homes for guillemot, razorbill, fulmar, shag, kittiwake and nesting gulls. In the past fishermen used to carry a spar up to Dun Cruit, lay this over the chasm and crawl across to collect the eggs and young birds.

A first visit to any strange anchorage is always a matter of concern. There are two approaches to Lunga and in blustery weather and a big sea we chose the easier – the north one. The sea is filled with spouting skerries and recognition of the right gap between them can be a problem. Leading beacons and the long spit with a castle-shaped rock may only reveal themselves when you are already committed to the fray. And yet the next visit is always so comparatively easy! We landed the dinghy on a beach of football-sized boulders and climbed to the plateau where the well-preserved remains of a line of black houses nestles in the nettles below Cruachan's north slope. A concealed fresh-water spring is in fairly close proximity and what appears to have been a walled vegetable patch takes advantage of a natural depression in the ground. Twenty people lived here in 1800 but Donald Campbell and his family were the last to leave in 1824. Loth to cut their ties so abruptly, however, the islanders returned each summer until 1857.

A rudimentary path runs round the entire island. About half-way along, rough man-made steps lead through the ferns into a mysterious silent cavern shaped like a circular pit with a dark narrow tunnel leading to the sea – what they call a 'gloup' in the Northern Isles.

The wild flowers on Lunga are too numerous to list here. Orchids speckle the grass with pink and examples of the rare oyster-plant can be seen. Dr Fraser Darling stayed for three months on Lunga in 1937 and only recorded two resident land mammals – rabbits and mice (apart from domestic sheep). He thought the mice were probably descendants of the house mice that had lived in the village a century before but his records were scanty as the mice ate them.

. . .these comic little birds. . .

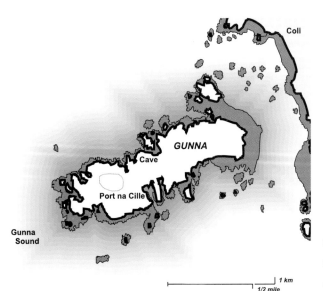

Coll

GUNNA

Cave

Port na Cille

Gunna
Sound

1 km
1/2 mile

GUNNA

. . . Some years ago about one hundred and sixty little whales, the biggest not exceeding twenty feet long, run themselves ashore in this isle, . . .very seasonably, in time of scarcity, for the natives did eat them all, and told me that the sea-pork, i.e., the whale, is both wholesome and very nourishing meat. . .

The bright morning had the promise of a hot day ahead as I bailed out some overnight rain from the dinghy. We were anchored in Clach Chuirr, a beautiful Tiree bay in the Sound of Gunna. There was a splash and two large dolphins surfaced within an arm's reach of me. They seemed amused by my efforts and for the next half-hour they played hide-and-seek, showing their white undersides in the clear water as they slipped under the dinghy or beneath *Jandara*'s keel.

Later they returned to accompany us across the sound to the low-lying island of Gunna. Adrian de Ferranti, whose brother Marcus is Gunna's owner, told us that the two friendly dolphins have been resident for the last six or seven years and love to greet boats as they sail by.

Gunna is one of our many small Scottish islands which is little known and usually ignored. It is narrow and wind-blown, no more than 500 metres wide for most of its length, less than 170 acres in area, and lies nearer to Coll then Tiree. A humpy bedrock of paragneiss schist is covered with a light soil and there are few prominent features except for a beautiful beach of clean Hebridean sand which partly surrounds the anchorage. The owner grazes about eighteen semi-wild cattle which swim over to Coll whenever the word 'abattoir' is mentioned in their presence, but the island grass is mainly cropped by large numbers of barnacle, white-fronted and greylag geese which bed-and-breakfast here. Their chipolata-shaped droppings are everywhere. Gulls and terns nest on the island but as it is such a short swim from Coll brown rats are reputed to mount occasional egg-raids.

We dropped anchor in the small bay on the east side of Eilean nan Gamhna, a tiny islet connected to Gunna at low water. The water was crystal clear and every link of the chain could be seen as the anchor dug in to the clean sandy bottom. The area in the immediate vicinity of Gunna is peppered with rocks and there are more rocky patches off the Tiree shore but most of the rocks can be easily identified whatever the state of the tide.

Gunna

Harry and Ronald explored the far side of the island while I walked across the tussocky grass to reconnoitre Port na Cille ('port of the chapel or cell'). This is a rocky inlet with a small square ruin which may have originally been the 'cille'. Latterly it was more likely to have been used as a small but superior-quality sheiling. It is beside a fresh-water spring which was dry due to a prolonged spell of dry weather. There are also other signs of summer sheilings but there is no official record of Gunna ever having been permanently inhabited. A level depression in the centre of the island – sheltered from the wind – could have been cultivated at one time and a distinctive cave in the centre of the north coast may once have served as an anchorite's shelter. The island was probably named after someone called Gunnar, Gunni or Gunn as these were common Scandinavian names.

From the highest point which is only just over thirty metres above sea level it is possible to look across the sound and see the entire spread of low-lying Tiree while to the southwest the distinctive volcanic shape of Bac Mór, the Dutchman's Cap, looks like a battleship bearing down on Iona. On my way back to the beach I met a botanist holding a clipboard on which she was noting and classifying the many varied species of wild flowers, grasses and mosses which grow in this lovely unspoilt environment.

After our walk in the hot sun we swam lazily in the shallows where the water was as warm as a South Sea lagoon before returning to the boat for a welcome 'sundowner'.

COLL

. . . is generally composed of little rocky hills covered with heath. The north side is arable ground, affording barley and oats; the inhabitants always feed on the latter, and those of Tiree on the former. The isle of Coll produces more boys than girls; as if nature intended both these isles for mutual alliances, without being at the trouble of going to the adjacent isles or continent to be matched. The Parish-Book, in which the number of the baptised is to be seen, confirms this observation.

For those who have travelled to Holland to see the world-famous tulip fields in bloom it may come as a surprise that our own Scottish island of Coll attempted to challenge Dutch horticultural supremacy. Much of the land in the north of the island is virtually empty – a large expanse of low-lying, rocky current buns peppered with lochans – but there is rich and fertile machair on the north-western coastal strip. This was the most densely populated part of the island in the 19th century until the area was deserted, not by forced clearance, but in protest against the imposition of increased rents by a new landlord. The vacant townships can still be seen and there are only a few occupied houses. It was this area of machair which was chosen for an imaginative experiment to grow tulips in competition with the Dutch. The climate is mild – Coll is one of the sunniest spots in Britain – and the flowers grew well, but the cost and difficulty of transportation apparently defeated the project. I can't help wondering though whether typical Dutch tenacity would not have found an answer!

Arinagour (which means the 'shieling of the goats' in Gaelic) is the ferry port and main anchorage. It is a charming place consisting mainly of two rows of trim whitewashed cottages which were built by Maclean, the laird of Coll, about 1800 in an attempt to modernise the island. Most of Arinagour's cottages are now holiday homes but on my last visit one genuine 'Collach' proudly showed me his potato patch – possibly the earliest potatoes in Scotland – which says something for the benign climate.

At the opposite end to the ferry pier, beyond the fuchsia hedges, is the friendly Isle of Coll Hotel with bicycles and mopeds for hire. Cycling is by far the best way to explore Coll's 19,000 acres: a car provides the sights, but not the scents and sounds. What a pity to miss the subtle smells of heather and hay, or seaweed on the ocean breeze, or the sound of a corncrake in the long grass – like a faulty electrical connection.

Arinagour, Coll

Whenever we are sailing south from Skye or the Small Isles and the low shape of Coll breaks the horizon I am reminded of Boswell's experience in October 1773 when he and Dr Johnson sailed from Skye bound for Iona. They had both been seasick and were approaching Ardnamurchan when the wind turned against them forcing McDonald, their skipper, to tack for Tobermory in the Sound of Mull. Boswell opted to stay on deck as conditions steadily worsened and night closed in. They made no progress against the wind and tide so the skipper eventually decided his only option was to try and make for Coll even though it was pitch dark by now, blowing a gale, and the anchorages on Coll were surrounded by dangerous rocks. 'Let us run for it in God's name,' said the skipper as the sails were in danger of being torn to pieces or the boat capsizing. Boswell admitted that by this time he was very frightened indeed and there was 'something grandly horrible' in the 'prodigious sea'. The ship was heeling alarmingly, 'sometimes to within an inch of the water'. As everyone on deck seemed to be very busy – the skipper was at the bow trying to spot the rocks, a one-eyed sailor was steering the vessel, and everyone was shouting loudly in Gaelic at the same time – Boswell asked what he could do to help. In the dark his hands were placed on a rope and he was told to grasp it very firmly as it might require to be pulled hard at any moment. For several hours he hung on grimly, soaked by sea and rain, waiting for the vital call to action which would allow him to save the ship. 'Amidst all these terrifying circumstances I endeavoured to compose my mind. It was not easy to do it. I thought of those who were dearest to me, and would suffer severely, should I be lost.'

It was only after the ship safely reached Coll and anchored that he realised, shamefacedly, that he had been merely hanging on to one of the shrouds – 'a rope which was fixed to the top of one of the masts'!

Port Mór, Muck

MUCK

*. . . It lies a little to the south-west of Rum, being four miles in circumference, all surrounded with
a rock; it is fruitful in corn and grass; the hawks in the rocks here are reputed to be very good. The
cattle, fowls, and amphibia of this island are the same as in other isles; the natives speak the Irish
tongue only, and use the habit worn by their neighbours. . .*

'Muck on the starboard bow,' says the old song and how often have we sailed straight
past with our eyes set on the Sgurr of Eigg or the awesome peaks of Rum. Yet this
modest little island, which can look from the distance like a low-lying green submarine,
has much to offer. Possibly its unattractive name is to blame for the lack of interest.

When Dr Samuel Johnson correctly addressed the Laird of Muck as 'Muck', the
Laird — with a touch of wishful thinking — asked to be called 'Monk' because,
he insisted, his property's original owner was a hermit from Iona. In the Gaelic
the name means 'isle of pigs' and the two drying islets off the north-west
shore also refer to livestock – 'island of the headland of the lambs' and 'horse
island', which has no horses but many nesting sea birds.

Muck's 1400 acres of fertile land were bought by the MacEwen family
in 1896 and they are still the resident owners. In Dr Johnson's time (1773)
about 140 people lived on the island in comparatively comfortable conditions. The laird was considerate and Boswell reported that he brought in a
surgeon to inoculate eighty of the younger residents against smallpox and
paid him half a crown per head for doing so. But by 1828 the population had
doubled and more than half the islanders were shipped off to Nova Scotia.

The MacEwen's have, happily, always struggled to maintain a viable
population on the island and they advertise at intervals for young settlers. Even
so, with a present population of just two dozen, the viability is marginal.

Although there is a Calmac passenger ferry service from Mallaig (and a private
service from Arisaig), visitors rarely visit this lovely peaceful island. It is exposed to
the Atlantic gales but these bring in the shell sands which make the basalt soil the
most fertile in the Small Isles. Most of the coast is rocky and near the west end there
are cliffs.

Lawrence MacEwen runs the main farm at Gallanach with his wife Jenny and some additional help. It is a mixed farm with sheep, some Rum ponies, a small dairy herd, delicious early potatoes, other root crops and oats. There are also two small tenant farms and the island is self-sufficient in milk, eggs and vegetables with the islanders having a communal vegetable patch for their own use. There are no cars, the farm tractor being the only powered transport, but then there are only two kilometres of road. As there is no peat, all fuel, apart from driftwood, has to be imported.

The four island children were taught in a corrugated iron shed with an outside lavatory until 1992 when Highland Regional Council approved the building of a new school. It cost over quarter of a million pounds but it has an indoor lavatory and a wind-powered electricity generator.

On one visit to Port Mór we had Ian's Scandinavian friends aboard and they claimed to feel a kinship with the island. The entrance is guarded by the 'red rock' and the 'black skerry' which demand reasonably careful navigation and don't give much protection from a southern swell, but this is the main harbour and it has a small settlement of houses and an all-important telephone box. Camping is allowed with permission and a guesthouse is run by Lawrence MacEwen's younger brother, Ewen. Freshly baked bread and rolls for breakfast and the occasional lobster are often on the menu. A ruined chapel is on the hill above Port Mór and on the south side of the harbour entrance a few remnants of an old Bronze Age fortification are still visible.

Otters play in Gallanach Bay on the north coast where sea-beans from the West Indies, which are considered lucky charms, are sometimes washed in by the Gulf Stream. In spite of the low height some alpine plants can be found growing on Muck – dwarf juniper, crowberry, club moss, rose root sedum, mountain cats-paw and pyramidal bugle. In early summer the fields are covered with marigold, iris, cornflower and bluebell but there is little heather. A few acres of woodland provide some welcome tree cover.

From the top of Ben Airean (137m), which is a gentle climb from Gallanach, the whole island reveals itself – with the great Sgurr of Eigg as a backdrop. Muck is not for strenuous pursuits. It is a place to ramble about and explore, and to revel in the ever-changing aspect of sea and sky.

EIGG

. . . There is a mountain in the south end, and on the top of it there is a high rock called Skur Egg, about an hundred and fifty paces in circumference, and has a fresh-water lake in the middle of it; there is no access to this rock but by one passage, which makes it a natural fort. . .

. . . There is a church here on the east side of the isle, dedicated to St Donnan, whose anniversary they observe. About thirty yards from the church there is a sepulchral urn under ground; it is a big stone hewn to the bottom, about four feet deep, and the diameter of it is about the same breadth; I caused them to dig the ground above it, and we found a flat thin stone covering the urn: it was almost full of human bones, but no head among them, and they were fair and dry. . . Some few paces to the north of the urn there is a narrow stone passage under ground, but how far it reaches they could give me no account. . .

Eigg is an island of dramatic contrasts. Viewed from the sea under a summer sun and blue sky, it could be Gauguin's choice, Tahiti – it even has its own palm trees. Seen from the land, on a hillwalk along the island's roof, the dazzling colours of a Gauguin painting are set off by Rum's dark mountains, Ainshval and Askival, towering into the clouds beyond the windswept sound. And from land or sea the scene is dominated by An Sgurr, the largest residual mass of columnar pitchstone lava in Britain, towering on the skyline to a height of nearly 400 metres above sea level.

Gauguin would have had a further affinity with Eigg. It used to be called Eilean Nimban More – the 'island of the mighty women' who were said to live on a crannog in a lochan beside An Sgurr. The present name, Eigg, is more prosaic. It's the Gaelic for a notch (*eag*) and viewed from Rum the silhouette shows a deep groove framed by the two humps of An Sgurr and An Cruachan.

The island has a very mixed geology. An Sgurr is a block of stone sitting on top of an ancient riverbed which is complete with driftwood fossils. The northern cliffs are sandstone which has eroded into fascinating shapes at Camus Sgiotaig where the beach is renowned for its Singing Sands (when dry the grains of white quartz drone eerily underfoot and when damp they squeak like blackboard chalk). At the north end fossilised fish and reptiles are to be found in shale at Eilean Tuilm just above the low-watermark.

In 1840 the fossilised remains of a Plesiosaur, a 180-million-year-old swimming 'Loch Ness Monster' with paddle-shaped legs and a long neck and tail, were found here.

Eigg has had a troubled history of ownership. St Donnan set up a sizeable monastery on the island but was murdered together with fifty-two of his monks in 617, some say by pirates, others by the warrior women who apparently disliked missionaries. At Kildonnan just north of the jetty an old Celtic cross-slab and the ruins of a church mark the site.

The Norsemen ruled Eigg until the MacDonalds seized it. They were granted legal title in 1309 by Bruce. An unhappy incident was said to have occurred in the winter of 1577 when raiding MacLeods from Skye were sent home castrated after being caught raping MacDonald girls on Eigg. The MacLeods were upset and retaliated in force. One hundred and ninety-five of the Eigg islanders hid in a cave (St Francis' Cave) but they were discovered by the MacLeods who lit a large brushwood fire at the entrance causing every MacDonald within the cave to die of suffocation. This cave is now also known as Massacre Cave. Another cave near it, called Cathedral Cave or MacDonalds' Cave was sometimes used for Catholic services, a custom dating from the persecution following the 1745 rebellion. A stone wall in the cave may have been an altar. Both caves are easily reached from the ferry jetty.

In 1829 the MacDonalds sold Eigg for £15,000 to an Aberdeen professor. At that time the population was about 500 but several clearances followed and conditions were bad until 1893 when a new owner, Robert Thompson, a wealthy shipbuilder, spent a lot of money on improvements. He was followed in the 1920s by James and Walter Runciman. They created the home farm and built 'The Lodge', a white Italian-style residence set in a garden of crazy-paving, catmint and carnations, and surrounded with semi-tropical palms, bamboo and lush woodland. This was a period of relative prosperity for the islanders.

After 1966 there were absentee landlords until 1975 when wealthy Keith Schellenberg moved in, and for some years all was well. But his relationship with the islanders gradually deteriorated and Schellenberg eventually sold out to a German artist called Maruma. Then in 1997 after a public appeal, the island's 7500 acres were purchased by the Isle of Eigg Heritage Trust, a body in which the islanders themselves have a share. I sincerely hope it works. There is plenty of faith but the future is still going to be very difficult. The statistics tell a story – there are only forty-nine adults (including relatively recent incomers) and twenty-one children – the highest proportion of children on any Scottish island – and there are no public services and no harbour – yet. The ferry has to call in at Galmisdale, where the ocean swell surges through the gap between the jetty and rocky Castle Island, and it cannot even lie alongside. Eigg is certainly going to need some mighty women.

The Sgurr of Eigg

RUM

. . . the north end produces some wood. The rivers on each side afford salmon. There is plenty of land and sea-fowl; some of the latter, especially the puffin, build in the hills as much as in the rocks on the coast, in which there are abundance of caves: the rock facing the west side is red, and that on the east side grey.

. . . The natives gave me an account of a strange observation, which they say proves fatal to the posterity of Lachlin, a cadet of MacLean of Coll's family; that if any of them shoot at a deer on the mountain Finchra, he dies suddenly, or contracts some violent distemper, which soon puts a period to his life. They told me some instances to this purpose: whatever may be in it, there is none of the tribe above-named will ever offer to shoot the deer in that mountain. . .

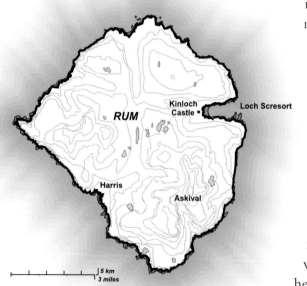

Whatever your political views it's impossible to deny that the world would be a much duller place without the wild antics of eccentric millionaires.

The Campbells of Oronsay, owners of the 25,000-acre island of Rum, had tried to farm sheep there without success and they were, therefore, only too happy in 1888 to sell this piece of midgy real estate to Mr John Bullough of Oswaldtwistle in Lancashire. He had made a great deal of money from the design and production of mill machinery and he was looking for a suitable holiday-retreat-cum-sporting-estate now that he was a Member of Parliament and a man of importance. Rum had been well-stocked with red deer and trout streams when the Marquis of Salisbury owned it for a spell in the 1850s so it was an ideal property for Mr Bullough. According to his widow he adored the island, and when he was out shooting he would often stop to write poetry while enjoying a cigar 'by some bonnie burn'.

He only lived for another three years to enjoy such pleasures and it was his eccentric twenty-one-year-old son, George, who inherited the estate in 1891. On coming into the family fortune George's first choice was to sail round the world on his father's steam-yacht. When he returned home he decided that Kinloch House, the laird's house on Rum which his father had used, was inadequate. He therefore commissioned London architects,

Kinloch Castle on Loch Scresort

Leeming & Leeming, to design him a castle fit for an island chieftain and to spare no expense. The design was eventually approved and work started on site in 1900. George shipped in red Arran sandstone and a squad of his local Lancashire stonemasons and issued them all with kilts. He had to pay extra to persuade the Englishmen to wear them and as they then complained that kilts left them exposed to the midges he supplemented their pay with 'midge-money' – tuppence a day to buy tobacco.

Kinloch Castle was completed in 1902. Garden soil was imported from Ayrshire so that the gardens could be pleasantly landscaped; grapes, figs, peaches and nectarines were grown in the glasshouses; special heated tanks were stocked with live turtles and alligators; the conservatory was filled with birds of paradise; and a large mechanical 'orchestrian' with trumpets and drums was installed to fill the castle with music (mainly military marches and operettas). There were double-glazed stained glass windows, central heating, a baronial hall, a billiard room with air-conditioning (to remove the cigar smoke), and a strange vertical 'jacuzzi' in the master bathroom complete with floral designs in the porcelain. Many of the exotic artefacts that he had collected on his world tour were used to furnish and decorate the castle.

Sir George Bullough was married on Rum and stayed there for three weeks every year. He was concerned that being called the Laird of Rum might be open to jest so he changed the spelling to Rhum. Thankfully, the traditional spelling has now been reinstated.

Guests were brought to Mallaig by a private train and taken by steam yacht to Loch Scresort on Rum where they were met at the pier by Albion motor cars and driven the short distance to the castle. Quite near the castle Sir George had built a special tomb with a white-tiled facade for his father's remains but as one of his guests was heard to remark that it looked like a London Underground lavatory he immediately built a mausoleum like a Greek temple in a distant glen and then dynamited the offending vault.

Sir George Bullough's widow, Monica Lady Bullough, sold Rum to the Government in 1957 for £26,000 and donated the castle's contents to the nation. The island's ecology and unique environment is now managed by Scottish Natural Heritage for the study and conservation of the natural flora and fauna including the red deer, Rum ponies, Highland cattle, and the reintroduced white-tailed sea-eagles. Much of the existing mixed woodland at Loch Scresort was planted by the Bulloughs but over one million native trees and shrubs have now been added as part of an extensive regeneration project. The castle itself is still splendid, but sadly subject to increasing deterioration. It badly needs renovation whether by an injection of Lottery cash – or the assistance of a reincarnated Sir George Bullough.

Rum is a magnificently wild place with dramatic scenery. Great mountains with glorious Norse names – Askival, Hallival, Trallval, and Ainshval – conceal remote and hidden glens, abrupt escarpments and boggy heathland. In 1957 the island was declared a National Nature Reserve and since then it has gained many more distinctions – National Scenic Area, Special Site of Scientific Interest, Specially Protected Area and Biosphere Reserve.

CANNA

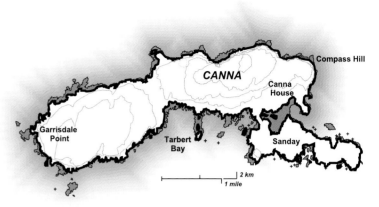

. . . There is a high hill in the north end, which disorders the needle in the compass. The stones in the surface of the earth are black, and the rock below facing the sea is red; some affirm that the needle of a ship's compass, failing by the hill, is disordered by the force of the magnet in this rock: but of this I have no certainty.

. . . There is good anchorage on the north-east of this isle. . .

This lovely island has one of the most popular anchorages on the West Coast; spacious and secure in any wind direction thanks to the protective arms of Canna and its connected little-sister island of Sanday. It also has a marvellous climate because the prevailing wind usually whips the clouds straight over to Rum where they hit the mountains and unload their rainy burden.

Having said that, on one of my earliest visits to Canna the rain was coming down so heavily that I almost had to swim through it. I had gone ashore to use the single lonely telephone box (which was painted blue) only to find the old press-button 'A or B' mechanism so jammed with coins that it was unusable and even dialling '100' for the operator drew a blank. I stood in that steamy box, expecting a fish to swim by at any moment and trying to think of a solution when I noticed, scratched among the graffiti, the word 'Try. . .' followed by a long number. I tried it, got a dialling tone, and then dialled my required number. Hey presto, I was immediately connected. Long distance, no charge – a Canna miracle!

Canna House, surrounded by thick woodland of native species such as rowan, hazel, ash, oak and birch, interspersed with some Corsican pine and Japanese larch, overlooks the harbour. It was the home of the late Dr John Lorne Campbell and his widow, the American writer Margaret Fay Shaw, who still lives there. Close by is the main farm with fields of delicious early potatoes or good old-fashioned haystacks creating a rural scene of yesteryear. A large herd of pedigree Highland cattle crop the fallow land and Cheviot sheep roam the hills.

In 1881 the island was bought by Robert Thom, a Glasgow shipowner, for £23,000. He was a benevolent landlord and in 1938 his family looked for a worthy successor. They chose

Haystacks on Canna

the Gaelic scholar, farmer and 'bonny fechter', John Lorne Campbell. He and Sir Compton Mackenzie had founded the 'Sea League' – a pressure group for the West Coast fishing industry – when they both lived on Barra in the 1930s. Campbell worked for most of his life on the preservation of Gaelic culture and he and his wife assembled the world's biggest library of Celtic literature and music. When in 1981 he, in turn, looked for a suitable guardian he chose to hand over Canna with its small community of about twenty islanders, and its priceless library, to the National Trust for Scotland.

It is worthwhile spending some time exploring this fascinating island because there is so much to see. A road runs west from the harbour beneath a basalt escarpment to Tarbert Bay where there is both a ruined fort and the remains of an ancient nunnery dating from the time when Canna belonged to Iona. On the north side of this central neck a well-preserved Viking ship burial was discovered and signs of Viking occupation are clearly visible. A rectangular outline of boulders is known as the grave of the King of Norway (Uaigh Righ Lochlainn).

Beyond Tarbert Bay the walk westwards to Garrisdale Point, with its two Iron Age forts and fortified wall, is more challenging as the track virtually disappears, but many of the most interesting features are quite close to the harbour and one of these is rarely seen by visitors. Through the gate, up the short hill-road beside the main farmhouse, and concealed by a hillock beyond the cemetery is the site of the original 19th-century 'township' with a broken Celtic cross of exquisite workmanship, remnants of an early 7th-century chapel, and, on a nearby hummock, a standing stone with a small hole in it at head height. This is called a pillory stone because, so we are told, an offender's thumb could be jammed in it!

The islanders are Catholic and worship in a modest building by the farmhouse. The ornate Catholic church standing on Sanday, the most conspicuous landmark on approaching the harbour, was built by Lady Bute in memory of her father but fell into serious disrepair. Happily, it is now being converted into a Gaelic Study Centre with accommodation for eighteen guests.

East of the harbour, near the ferry pier, is a charming little Protestant church, constructed in 1914 as a memorial to Robert Thom, with a conical bell tower and vaulted roof like early Celtic churches. Behind it is an unusual rocky pinnacle with a medieval prison tower on top where a Clanranald chief imprisoned his wife to keep her from her lover – a MacLeod from Skye.

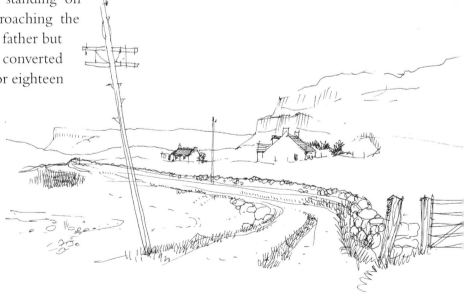

BERNERAY

. . . Berneray. . . excels other islands of the same extent for cultivation and fishing. The natives never go a fishing while Macneil or his steward is in the island, lest seeing their plenty of fish, perhaps they might take occasion to raise their rents.

. . . The natives endure a great fatigue in manuring their ground with sea- ware, which they carry in ropes upon their backs over high rocks. They likewise fasten a cow to a stake, and spread a quantity of sand on the ground, upon which the cow's dung falls, and this they mingle together, and lay it on the arable land.

. . . There is a sort of stone in this island, with which the natives frequently rub their breasts by way of prevention, and say it is a good preservative for health. This is all the medicine they use. Providence is very favourable to them, in granting them a good state of health, since they have no physician among them.

. . . The inhabitants are very hospitable, and have a custom, that when any strangers. . . resort thither, the natives, immediately after their landing, oblige them to eat, even though they should have liberally eaten and drank but an hour before their landing there. . . And whatever number of strangers come there, or of whatsoever quality or sex, they are regularly lodged according to ancient custom, that is, one only in a family; by which custom a man cannot lodge with his own wife. . .

Sail as far south as you can in the Outer Hebrides and you reach Berneray – proud and tall where she faces the storm-swept Atlantic. If your idea of paradise is a distant isle on the edge of a limitless ocean – and never mind the weather – then this could be it. Berneray is also known as Barra Head to avoid confusion with the other Berneray in the Sound of Harris. A century ago her 500 acres supported a population of over seventy but by 1931 three lighthouse keepers and their wives were the only occupants and now even they have gone.

Although there is a small stone and concrete jetty, landing can be difficult. We anchored *Jandara* east of Shelter Rock and Ian controlled our dinghy well as the surge carried us in but it was impossible to get a grip on the seaweed-covered slope and in the end he put

Bothy on Berneray

Peter and me ashore at a nearby rocky cleft occupied by a bewildered grey seal. We followed the vehicle track which climbs up the hill from the landing place to the whitewashed lighthouse at the summit. It was early May and the hillside was a riot of colour with primroses, celandine, wild violets and yellow flag iris – luckily not the chosen diet for the 200 or so breeding ewes which are kept here by the owners – a syndicate of Barra crofters.

Barra Head lighthouse was built with granite quarried on the island but unfortunately its siting resulted in the destruction of the greater part of an Iron Age galleried dun or fortress. A gateway now leads from the lighthouse yard through the ancient wall to a cliff-top area completely surrounded by a natural parapet of stone slabs and boulders. From here the precipice drops vertically to the surging waves over 180 metres below. Alongside, there is a great chasm – Sloc na Beiste ('ravine of the monster') – leading to a cave which is concealed from view. The roar of the sea breaking into the chasm far below forms a bass chorus to the cries of thousands of wheeling seabirds and the wind whistling up the cleft takes your breath away.

These magnificent cliffs take the full force of gigantic seas because there is no shallow water to impede them. The lighthouse keepers recorded that small fish were often found in the grass at the top after severe gales and as proof of the ferocity of the wind and sea it was reliably reported in 1836 that a forty-two ton rock was moved almost five feet during a violent storm.

Berneray, which is one of the group of islands known as the Bishop's Isles, traditionally belonged to MacNeil of Barra. Fresh water can be scarce, and in dry summers the islanders had to ship water over from neighbouring Mingulay. There is a 'chalybeate spring' (water with traces of iron in it) about halfway up the track, with a small pumphouse to provide water for the lighthouse. A helicopter pad near the top allows maintenance teams to service the lighthouse now that it is automatic.

Apart from the site of a chapel (near the landing place), Berneray has five cists, five suspected burial cairns and four megalithic chamber tombs, so the island appears to have been well occupied as far back as the Neolithic/ Bronze Age.

MINGULAY

. . .When a tenant's wife in this or the adjacent islands dies, he then addresses himself to Macneil of Barra representing his loss, and at the same time desires that he would be pleased to recommend a wife to him, without which he cannot manage his affairs, nor beget followers to Macneil, which would prove a public loss to him. Upon this representation, Macneil finds out a suitable match for him; and the woman's name being told him, immediately he goes to her, carrying with him a bottle of strong waters for their entertainment at marriage, which is then consummated.

. . .When a tenant dies, the widow addresseth herself to Macneil in the same manner, who likewise provides her with a husband, and they are married without any further courtship.

. . . If a tenant chance to lose his milk-cows by the severity of the season, or any other misfortune; in this case Macneil of Barra supplies him with the like number that he lost.

. . .When any case of these tenants are so far advanced in years that they are incapable to till the ground, Macneil takes such old men into his own family, and maintains them all their life after. . .

In the old days when the MacNeil of Barra was laird of Mingulay his annual rent was mainly *fachaich* – shearwater chicks collected by the islanders from the precipices. The story goes that on one occasion when MacNeil's rent collector, Macphee, landed on Mingulay he found everyone dead. He rushed back to the boat and called to the men to take him off quickly as there was 'plague' on the island. On hearing this the men rowed away and left him marooned with only the corpses for company. Every day he would climb the hill to the north of the village and signal frantically to passing ships but they would just wave back and pass on. He survived for more than a year and eventually MacNeil decided it was safe to have the island resettled. By way of friendly compensation he made a special grant of land to Macphee including the hill which, since then, has always been known as Macphee's Hill.

When we first anchored in Village Bay it was a perfect day in late April and with the great stretch of white beach, a warm sun and a turquoise sea it could have been the South Seas.

Mingulay which, at nearly 1600 acres, is the largest of the group of islands south of Barra, is almost another St Kilda. Its towering cliffs and stacks face the Atlantic while the east side

AN ISLAND
ODYSSEY

—

Mingulay

slopes gradually down to a rugged foreshore. Mingulay Bay (or Village Bay) is centrally situated on the more-sheltered east coast and the extensive remains of the deserted village straddle the valley burn. In the 1800s the population rose to about 150 but with overcrowding, epidemics, and the lack of a pier, the islanders started to look elsewhere. Desperation, daring, and eventual success rewarded those who 'raided' land on Vatersay and Sandray. Numbers dwindled rapidly, fell below a sustainable level, and the last inhabitants left in 1912.

The schoolhouse built in the 1880s at the south end of the bay by the Free Church Ladies' Association has been used as a bothy and fank since the first sheep-farmer, Jonathan MacLean, took over in 1912. At the opposite end – above the village ruins – stands the Catholic priest's house which is still roofed. It was built in 1898 and had a chapel on the upper floor. The valley west of the village was extensively cultivated and the old runrig field divisions can still be seen. Patches of cultivation and lazybeds are also to be seen near the coastline stretching round to Skipisdale on the south coast where there was also some habitation.

Normally the great Atlantic rock-faces can only be seen clearly from the sea but an interesting walk up the valley which I took with Peter arrives at a point above Bàgh na h-Aoineig ('bay of the steep promontory'), a gigantic cleft cutting deep into the island. From here it is possible to look across the cleft and see the utterly breathtaking height of the precipice rising straight out of the sea and soaring towards the sky. Near the top it leans further and further out in a great rock cornice which looks as though it might overbalance at any moment. During the breeding season every little horizontal crack, ledge and crevice is stippled white with kittiwakes, razorbills and guillemots – each insignificant dot another nesting bird. Sheep were grazed on the grassy tops of the two famous stacks, Arnamul (Old Norse for 'erne mound') and Lianamul ('flax mound'), which stand close to the cliffs on either side of Bàgh na h-Aoineig. For many years Lianamul, which has a sea cave, was reached by a rope bridge spanning the chasm but this had disappeared by 1871. Before the bridge was constructed the people would climb to the top of Lianamul 'at the risk of their lives, and by means of a horse-hair rope carry up their wedders to fatten'. It is possible to sail a small boat through a huge natural rock arch near Arnamul on the rare occasions when conditions are suitable.

These sea cliffs tower up to a height of over 220 metres and are among the most dramatic in the British Isles. The greatest sheer drop is 'Biulacraig' which is also the Clan MacNeil war-cry.

After Peter and I had explored the cliff-tops and returned hot and weary to find Ian asleep in the sun we all set about launching the dinghy. Each time we jumped aboard a wave swept us back up the beach. We eventually succeeded, but not before we had gained a new sympathy for poor old Macphee.

Opposite: The chasm of Arnamul

A puffer at Castlebay, Barra

BARRA

. . . There is a safe harbour on the north-east side of Barra, where there is great plenty of fish.

The rivers on the east side afford salmon. . . The natives go with three several herring nets, and lay them crossways in the river where the salmon are most numerous, and betwixt them and the sea. These salmon at the sight or shadow of the people make towards the sea, and feeling the net from the surface to the ground, jump over the first, then the second, but being weakened, cannot get over the third net, and so are caught. They delight to leap above water and swim on the surface. One of the natives told me that he killed a salmon with a gun, as jumping above water.

They informed me also that many barrels of them might be taken. . . if there was any encouragement for curing and transporting them. . .

Some years ago tobacco did grow here, being of all plants the most grateful to the natives, for the islanders love it mightily. . .

The little island Kismul. . . is the seat of Macneil of Barra; there is a stone wall round it two stories high, reaching the sea, and within the wall there is an old tower and a hall, with other houses about it. I saw the officer called the Cockman, and an old cock he is; when I bid him ferry me over the water to the island, he told me that he was but an inferior officer, his business being to attend in the tower; but if (says he) the constable, who then stood on the wall, will give you access, I'll ferry you over. I desired him to procure me the constable's permission, and I would reward him; but having waited some hours for the constable's answer, and not receiving any, I was obliged to return without seeing this famous fort. . .

I was told some weeks after that the constable was very apprehensive of some design I might have in viewing the fort, and thereby to expose it to the conquest of a foreign power, of which I supposed there was no great cause of fear . . .

Many years ago a brisk south-easterly chased *Jandara* across the Hebridean Sea to Barra where horizontal bands of sleet swept Castlebay. The only sheltered anchorage – behind the little castle which rises abruptly out of the sea – was very crowded but we squeezed in with little swinging room to spare. A line of derelict petrol tankers and a beached trawler seemed to litter the main street and there was no sign of life whatsoever.

'I'm from Uist,' said the barman.

'So why did you come to Barra?' Ian asked.

'For the activity,' he said seriously.

I came to understand the remark on a more recent visit when the hot sun brought out the tourists in droves. Café tables on the pavements gave Castlebay a Continental flavour. Harry and Brenda suggested a cycle run round the island and Ronald, who cycles regularly, concurred. The helpful lassie who hired us well-maintained bikes assured us we would enjoy the run but warned us of – 'a *tehrible* hill!' We chose a clockwise circuit and set off past the unbelievably beautiful white-sand bays of the west coast and then turned across the north of the island where the road winds through the dry bracken hillsides by Loch an Dùin. Ronald and I were ahead when North Bay came in sight so we sat down by the roadside on a smooth granite outcrop. Harry and Brenda soon joined us to take a rest and admire the view when a girl came out of a house carrying a tray with four cups and saucers, a steaming teapot, milk, sugar and biscuits.

'We thought you might feel like a cup of tea,' she said with a smile.

Where else in the world, in this day and age, could one find such friendly and hospitable people? That gesture lit up our whole afternoon – it was not only the sun that was shining! From then on everyone we passed seemed to give us a cheerful wave and wish us well. We pedalled happily up the slopes and, without a care in the world, freewheeled down again by white cottages clustered in rocky inlets. The mountains of Hartaval and Heaval towered above us. And then the road started winding up the flank of Heaval and out of sight and we fell off our saddles and started the long walk home. At each bend another upward stretch revealed itself. 'Yes,' we would say seriously to anyone who listened, 'it's a *tehrible* hill.'

Some say that the chiefs of the Clan MacNeil who inhabit Kisimul Castle can be traced back to Niall of the Nine Hostages, the 4th-century High King of Ireland. But it is at least on record that they were granted a charter to Barra in the 15th century by both the Lord of the Isles and James IV. Within a few decades they were using Kisimul Castle in Castle Bay as a pirate base for raids on the ships of the English Queen Elizabeth. MacNeil explained to James VI that this was justifiable because 'that woman' had killed the king's mother (Mary Queen of Scots). As the Earl of Argyll commented on receiving a letter from MacNeil of Barra – 'His style of letter runs as if he were of another kingdom.'

But piracy had to cease and by 1838 the chief, General Roderick MacNeil, was so heavily in debt that he sold the island to Colonel Gordon of Cluny for £38,050. On the grounds of receiving insufficient rent Cluny imported mainland policemen and cleared the island of its crofters, stole their stock and belongings, and sent them penniless to the New World. When the colonel died in 1858 Barra and its few survivors passed to Lady Gordon Cathcart and her husband, who did nothing to improve matters. It was only in 1937 that most of Barra was bought back by the present MacNeil's father, an American architect and the Clan's forty-fifth chieftain. He restored the castle which had been uninhabited for more than 200 years and made it a place of pilgrimage for the clan. The present chief, Ian MacNeil, teaches law in Chicago. A flag flies when he is in residence at Kisimul and the castle can be visited by the public.

A few years ago, in the shadow of Kisimul Castle, I was pleased to see the gallant little puffer *Eilean Eisdeal* busily offloading coal into a lop-sided lorry. She was one of the last – if not the last – of the Para Handy line, complete with empty whisky bottle rolling in the gunnel. But a very sad sight greeted us last summer when passing the small island of Easdale – the puffer lay there, dead, beached and deserted.

The secret anchorage

HELLISAY

. . . Some isles lie on the east and north of Barray, as Fiaray, Mellisay, Buya Major and Minor, Lingay, Fuda. . .

This island, and the adjacent lesser islands, belong in property to Macneil, being the thirty-fourth of that name by lineal descent. . . He holds his lands in vassalage of Sir Donald Macdonald of Sleat, to whom he pays £40 per annum and a hawk, if required, and is obliged to furnish him a certain number of men upon extraordinary occasions.

. . . The steward is reckoned a great man here, in regard of the perquisites due to him; such as a particular share of all the lands, corn, butter, cheese, fish, etc., which these islands produce; the measure of barley paid him by each family yearly is an omer, as they call it, containing two pecks.

. . . There is an inferior officer, who also hath a right to a share of all the same products. Next to these come in course those of the lowest posts, such as the cockman and porter, each of whom hath his respective due, which is punctually paid. . .

Hellisay, and its sister island Gighay, are separated from each other by a narrow sound and a concealed central 'lagoon'. We were very keen to explore this area but the entire passage is strewn with rocks, a two-knot spring tide tumbles over the shallow sand bars and the charts don't claim to be accurate. We timed our arrival for an hour before high water so that *Jandara*'s keel could cross the sand bar but, of course, this meant that most of the rocks had disappeared below the surface. The narrow entry also has a concealed bend which is daunting, but we inched our way through without mishap and scraped over the sandbar. Suddenly the land closed behind us like a door and we were trapped in a secret world. Grey seals stared at us in surprise, oyster-catchers raised objections, an eagle circled over the cliffs, and the surrounding shores were bright with marsh marigold and yellow flag iris.

We anchored first beside an islet off Gighay called Hundred Island (Eilean a' Ceud) and went ashore. Only the broken sheep pens beneath the bluff betray the presence of man but among the nettles and bracken there are the remains of a dozen or so, small, rude, stone dwellings and, on the opposite slope, the regular striations of old lazybeds are just visible.

Squally gusts of breeze were sweeping down the hillside so for better shelter we decided to move over to the opposite side at Hintish Bay on Hellisay. By now the tide was falling – but the rocks were still concealed.

I usually end up as navigator on our expeditions – probably because I'm an architect ('He can read plans!') – and I must admit that I enjoy the challenge, but navigation when rocks are hidden and the 'plans' are unreliable is not a scientific operation. Our chosen anchorage was very close to a reef but there was no visible sign of it whatsoever. Ian was on the helm and Peter at the bow as we slipped slowly across the bay and I tried to judge the reef's position. At last I felt we were as close to it as we dared to go and Peter let go the anchor. We seemed to have a good hold so we decided to call it a day and went below.

The next morning was sparkling bright, the wind had dropped and nothing disturbed the perfect reflections on the water. The rocks were once again covered by the tide. I took the dinghy ashore on Hellisay to sketch the scene and landed on a narrow neck of land dividing the stillness and perfection of our private lagoon from the busy world outside. On the one side there was not a ripple on the water, on the other side the restless sea was surging into a narrow rock cleft with a noise like severe indigestion. Peter joined me later and we scrambled up the eighty metres or so to the top of Meall Mór and Meadhonach. From there the whole Sound of Barra lay before us and its many islands with delightful alliterative names like Flodday, and Fuiay, and Fiaray. We could see Bualavore at the western end of Hellisay where more than 100 people desperately tried to start a new life when they were cleared from the adjoining islands in the early 1800s. They built shelters for their families and eked out a meagre living only to find that, less than a generation later, they were once again to be driven from their homes. Many of these islanders from Hellisay and Gighay then found refuge on Eriskay but many also gave up the unequal struggle and headed for the New World. A short visit here is delightful, particularly in fine weather, but the islanders' existence must have been tenuous. These islands are barren enough in spring and summer – what can it be like during the long winter months? Only the inland sea, sheltered between the islands, could possibly tip the scales by providing all-weather fishing with nothing but seals for competition.

By the time we had returned to *Jandara* the tide was out and all the rocks were revealed. *Jandara* lay, as planned, close to the reef. So close in fact that lying innocently on its seaweed-covered top, which was now level with our deck, was our anchor!

ERISKAY

The island Erisca, about a mile in length, and three in circumference, is partly heathy and partly arable, and yields a good produce. The inner side hath a wide anchorage, there is excellent cod and ling in it; the natives begin to manage it better, but not to that advantage it is capable of. . .

It's a good one-and-a-half miles walk from the Big Harbour to the friendly bar in Am Politician – the local pub on Eriskay. The landscape is harsh, treeless, unforgiving – far removed from the soft romanticism of the beautiful *Eriskay Love-Lilt*.

Halfway along we passed a wrecked and rusting car which still had a sign in its rear window – 'I love Eriskay' – and below the narrow road we could see the Prince's Strand – the beach where, on 23rd July 1745, Prince Charles Edward Stuart was put ashore from the French ship *Du Teillay* for the start of his ill-fated Scottish venture.

The pub is in one of the most Scandinavian-type settlements in Scotland – trim brightly coloured houses scattered almost at random over the north of the island – but you have to add a clutter of wires and telephone poles and a house which is painted from top to bottom with bright green and white horizontal stripes (Celtic is the popular team).

The name Eriskay actually means 'the island of the water-nymph' but that seemed inapt when we entered the pub as it was crowded – filled with the sound of soft Gaelic voices and the sweet smell of golden spirit.

When the notorious Colonel Gordon of Cluny bought the island in 1838, together with Barra, Benbecula and South Uist, he allowed a few of the crofters whom he had evicted from Uist to settle on Eriskay because the land was considered too barren even for sheep to survive. As a consequence the population of Eriskay shot up from 80 to over 450. Many crofters preferred destitution in Scotland to penniless emigration to Nova Scotia so they built raised lazybeds of peat and seaweed on the rocky ground and grew meagre crops of barley, oats and potatoes. It was a battle for survival. Those who could acquire a small boat were able to fish and eventually this became the main occupation and the community gained a modicum of prosperity.

On 5th February 1941, when Hitler's U-boats were exacting a terrible toll on merchant shipping in the Battle of the Atlantic, the 12,000-ton SS *Politician* sailing from Liverpool to New York foundered in the Sound of Eriskay and broke in two. She was trying to avoid attention by sneaking through the Minch but should never have ventured into the shallow sound. Part of her assorted cargo was 264,000 bottles of whisky so as soon as the crew was safely ashore the islanders felt it their duty to ensure that this precious cargo was not lost at sea. The good work proceeded happily for several weeks until, to the islanders' surprise, HM Customs & Excise appeared on the scene with some police and demanded the return of the cargo. This was the part of the story which Sir Compton Mackenzie wove into his classic tale *Whisky Galore!* But the rest of the true story was not so amusing because, although the local police disliked the affair and would have nothing more to do with it, the excisemen sent thirty-six islanders to court including a fourteen-year old boy. Nineteen were found guilty of illegal possession and imprisoned at Inverness.

Some 'polly-pottles' – as they are called on the island – still occasionally turn up in the most unexpected hidey-holes. They can be easily recognised because they are stamped – 'No resale without Federal approval'.

A former Catholic priest of Eriskay who was born on South Uist, Father Allan McDonald, is remembered for his valuable collection of Gaelic folk-tales, his dictionary of Gaelic phrases, and his poetry. He died in 1905 at the early age of forty-six, a simple man and a dedicated scholar. Unfortunately, much of his literary work was mutilated by a German woman, Ada Goodrich-Freer, who befriended him, persuaded him to hand over his manuscripts and then published much of the material (incorrectly edited) under her own name.

It was drizzling when we left the pub but the landscape had taken on a mellow look, the hills on Barra were plum-coloured against the western sky, and the Big Harbour was much closer than we had imagined.

Eriskay, which has been one of the most thriving small communities in the Outer Hebrides, is facing an uncertain future. It is the inevitable island problem of communications not meeting present-day standards and people are starting to leave. Access by ferry from South Uist is limited, expensive, and subject to the tides as the sound is so shallow. A causeway is desperately needed: but who is prepared to pay for it?

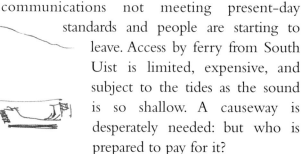

Haun, Eriskay

The Monachs in the mist

THE MONACH ISLES

. . . the island of Heiskir which lies near three leagues westward of North Uist, is three miles in circumference, of a sandy soil, and very fruitful in corn and grass, and black cattle. The inhabitants labour under want of fuel of all sorts, which obliges them to burn cow's dung, barley-straw, and dried sea-ware; the natives told me that bread baked by the fuel of sea-ware relishes better than that done otherwise.

. . . There are two small islands separated by narrow channels from the north-west of this island. . . The natives say that there is a couple of ravens there, which suffer no other of their kind to approach. . . and if any such chance to come this couple immediately drive them away. . . The natives told me that when one of this couple happened to be wounded by gun-shot, it lay still in the corner of a rock for a week or two, during which time its mate brought provision to it daily until it recovered perfectly. The natives add further that one of these two ravens having died some time after, the surviving one abandoned the island for a few days, and then was seen to return with about ten or twelve more of its kind, and having chosen a mate out of this number, all the rest went quite off, leaving these two in possession of their little kingdom. . .

The Monach Isles, situated out in the Atlantic about five miles west of North Uist, are really no more than a group of sand dunes on a rocky base with a maximum height of less than twenty metres above sea level. The Norse called the largest of the group Heisker, the bright skerry, probably from the colour of the sand when the sun glints on it. History records that there was once a great stretch of sandbank which was exposed at low water and which linked the entire group to North Uist. In other words this was really a peninsula projecting out into the Atlantic although the distance would probably have precluded any chance of walking across it between the tides. But in the 16th century an enormous tsunami – a tidal wave – swept away the sand banks and the Monach Isles and their inhabitants have been isolated ever since. More recent examples have shown what utter devastation a tsunami or tidal wave can cause but history does not record in this instance how many of the islanders, if any, survived the disaster.

In spite of the risks of living in such a frail and exposed environment human settlement certainly goes back to before AD1000 and the average population was probably somewhere between 70 and 100. But in 1810 the islands were abandoned because overgrazing had destroyed the machair and exposed large areas of sand. Before the ground could recover there was a great storm which tore up the remaining turf and covered the islands with even more sand. Thirty years later a small group of about thirty-nine islanders returned, probably due to pressure from the clearances of the larger islands. They planted marram grass to stabilise the soil and once again the Monachs were in business. By 1861 the population had risen to 127.

By 1931, the usual pressures on small island communities had taken their toll. The young people who travelled 'abroad' failed to return, numbers steadily dwindled and the remaining thirty-three islanders moved over to North Uist for good. Only the lighthouse keepers stayed on for a few more years.

The Gaelic name – the Monach Isles – means 'the islands of the monks'. Three linked islands form the main group. In about the 13th century a nunnery or convent having connections with Iona was established on Ceann Ear ('east head'), the largest part of the main group. Later, a monastery was built on Shillay, a separate small flanking island on the west side. Part of the monks' duties was to maintain a light as a guide for mariners. (This site, incidently, also kept the monks a decorous distance away from the nuns.) The Monachs monastic associations were abandoned about the time of the Reformation although the islands continued to be populated. In 1864 a red brick lighthouse was built on Shillay to replace the old monks' light but this was abandoned in 1942. A dressed stone taken from this lighthouse had the words 'Eternity oh eternity' carved on it by a lighthouse keeper.

The remains of some patches of grazing and cultivated land can still be seen in the vicinity of the small village on Ceann Ear which is situated near Loch nam Buadh – the loch of virtues. The village, which is now disintegrating, had good amenities, a post-office and a school, but no shops.

The Monachs had a tenuous connection with the Jacobite Rebellion. The bad-tempered wife of Lord James Erskine of Grange, known as Lady Grange, was in her drawing room in Edinburgh in 1731 when her husband brought in some conspirators for a meeting. Curiosity overcame discretion and instead of leaving the room she hid behind a settee. After she had heard the discussion she stupidly stood up and threatened to denounce them. The conspirators decided she must be silenced so her death was announced and Edinburgh society attended her elaborate 'funeral' at Greyfriars Church. Meanwhile she was secretly whisked away to the Monach Isles where she was held prisoner until 1734 before being transferred to St Kilda. She was treated well but was said to have spent her time wandering about all night, weeping loudly, and throwing letters into the sea tied to corks. After eight years she was moved to Skye and taught how to weave and it was there that she died in 1745. As the authorities had learned that she might still be alive, the conspirators covered their trail further by staging two separate funerals in different places thus making her possibly the only person ever to have had three funerals!

HIRTA

. . . faced all round with a steep rock, except the bay on the south-east, which is not a harbour fit for any vessel, though in the time of a calm one may land upon the rock, and get up into the island with a little climbing.

. . . Both men and women are well-proportioned. . . Both sexes have a lisp, but more especially the women, neither of the two pronouncing the letters, d, g, or r. There are some of both sexes who have a genius for poetry, and are great admirers of musick; the trump or Jewish harp is all the musical instrument they have, which disposes them to dance mightily. Their sight is extraordinary good… they have very good memories, and are resolute in their undertakings, chaste and honest, and the men reputed jealous of their wives. They argue closely. . . are reputed very cunning, and. . . they marry very young, the women at about thirteen or fourteen years of age. The most ancient person among them at present, is not above eighty. . .

. . . There is this only wanting to make them the happiest people in this habitable globe, viz., that they themselves do not know how happy they are, and how much they are above the avarice and slavery of the rest of mankind. . .

This is surely a dream destination for all those who love wild, romantic, far-away places: a distant isle in the wild Atlantic once peopled by a hardy and self-sufficient race who had survived successfully for several thousand years only to be wiped out in a few decades by the intrusion of modern civilisation.

Most people call Hirta 'St Kilda' but the name of St Kilda actually applies to the whole archipelago – Hirta, Boreray, Soay, Dun, and a number of isolated rocks and stacks. The island of Hirta is the largest of the group, and probably the only one which was ever permanently inhabited. Its awesome cliffs and peaks actually make it look larger than it really is: at less than 1700 acres in area it is smaller than Iona or Scarba.

The origin of the name St Kilda is a puzzle as there is no record of any saint of that name. One possible explanation is that just above the village 'street' in Village Bay there is a spring of clear water set among mossy stones and clumps of flag iris. This was the village's main source of fresh water and I can vouch for its clean and sparkling taste. Along came the Norsemen looking for fresh water for their ships and they asked the locals what they called the spring. 'Tobar,' was the reply, which simply means a 'spring' or 'well' in Gaelic (e.g. Tobermory – the well of St Mary). So the Norsemen called it the 'tobar spring' or *tobar kelda* in Norse. We all make this mistake when two or more languages are involved. For instance, Edinburgh Castle means 'Edin's Castle Castle' and the famous Eas Fors Waterfall on Mull means 'waterfall waterfall waterfall'! The St Kildans eventually adopted the same name – Tobar Childa – in order to distinguish this important well from another one to the east of the village. Then the Dutch came along and produced the first map of the Western

Tobar Childa – a spring of clear water

Isles in 1666. They knew that most Scottish wells were associated with saints and therefore assumed that the island's patron saint must be St Kilda.

The first impression on arriving in Village Bay is of an ancient Stone Age settlement. Everything seems to be of stone and everywhere you look there are stone structures – houses, dykes and hundreds of the primitive storage cells called 'cleits' like petrified pimples on the mountain slopes. The amount of rock shifting that has taken place through the centuries is quite remarkable. The line of village houses which is being lovingly restored today by the owner, the National Trust for Scotland, is relatively modern. The original village was demolished in 1830 and black houses were built instead but these were partly replaced only thirty years later by the present line of typical 'but and bens' built with mortar and to Victorian standards.

To add to the Stone Age atmosphere, wild sheep with evil eyes and scruffy umber-coloured fleeces crop the grass among the stones or chew their cud in the shelter of the dykes. These primitive sheep – one of the very earliest types – were not to be seen on Hirta when the islanders were evacuated in August 1930 because the St Kildans had always kept them on the neighbouring island of Soay (which means 'sheep island' in Old Norse). But some were brought over to Hirta a few years after the evacuation and these are now being studied by scientists of Scottish Natural Heritage.

Archaeologists think that Hirta may have been continuously inhabited for about 3500 years although where the original St Kildans came from is

'High Street', Village Bay

anybody's guess. They appear to have lived a tough, basic, but relatively contented life with a population of possibly 150 to 200 and almost all their needs provided by the sea birds, the product of their lazybeds, and some livestock. Produce such as tweed, wool, feathers or fulmar oil was paid as rent to MacLeod of Harris and collected once a year by a steward. (It was reported that the only time they ever caught a cold was when the steward appeared.) This visit was virtually the only contact with the rest of the world until the 18th century when visiting ships introduced cholera and smallpox which reduced the population to about seventy.

Then in 1834 the first tourist ship, the *Glen Albyn*, called at the island and this marked the start of the end of St Kilda. Many tourists followed, often cheating the naïve islanders, and to make matters worse a hell–fire and damnation minister arrived and persuaded them to spend long hours every day in church instead of working. The result was inevitable.

I am sure every visitor must view this astonishing island with mixed emotions. A rusted iron pot or a scrap of rope on the floor of a cleit are sad ghosts of the past. Wrens chirping in the sunlight, buttercup meadows brushed by Atlantic breezes and the overpowering beauty of nature offer utter delight with the present.

BORERAY

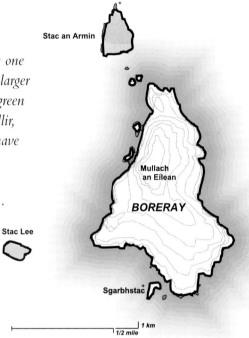

Stac an Armin

Mullach
an Eilean

BORERAY

Stac Lee

Sgarbhstac

1 km
1/2 mile

. . .This isle is very high and all rock, being inaccessible except in a calm, and there is only one place for landing, looking to the south: in the west end. . . is Stallir-House, which is much larger than that of the female warrior in St Kilda, but of the same model in all respects; it is all green without like a little hill; the inhabitants there have a tradition that it was built by one Stallir, who was a devout hermit of St Kilda; and had he travelled the universe he could scarcely have found a more solitary place for a monastick life. . .

. . .There was an earthquake here in the year 1686, which lasted but a few minutes; it was very amazing to the poor people, who never felt any such commotion before, or since. . .

. . .To the west of Borera lies the rock Stack-Narmin, within pistol-shot; there is a possibility of landing only in two places, and that but in a perfect calm neither, and after landing the danger in climbing it is very great. . .The sea rises and rages extraordinarily upon this rock: we had the curiosity, being invited by a fair day, to visit it for pleasure, but it was very hazardous to us; the waves from under our boat rebounding from off the rock, and mounting over our heads wet us all, so that we durst not venture to land, though men with ropes were sent before us; and we thought it hazard great enough to be near this rock; the wind blew fresh, so that we had much difficulty to fetch St Kilda again. . .

This must be Scotland's most dramatic island – a quite remarkable, jagged heap of black volcanic rock rearing 386 metres (1260 feet) above the sea. It is an unforgettable sight, particularly when the cloud swirls around its summit and the gannets plunge from breathtaking heights. It is an island of superlative emotions that change with the weather. In the words of the yachtsman, RA Smith, who sailed there in *Nyanza* in 1879: 'Had it been a land of demons it could not have appeared more dreadful'. The name, Boreray, comes from the Old Norse meaning 'island like a fortress' which is very apt.

Boreray lies about three-and-a-half miles to the north-east of Hirta with two enormous stacks standing guard beside it, Stac an Armin and Stac Lee. It is possible to sail between Boreray and Stac Lee – quite an experience – but the channel between Boreray and Stac an Armin is littered with rocks and should not be attempted. I have never landed on Boreray and probably never will as considerable mountaineering skill is required. Above the only landing place, which is near Sgarbhstac ('cormorant stack'), there is a chasm of nearly two metres width at the narrowest point. It is necessary to jump across this onto a slippy foothold with the sea surging thirty metres below in order to start the hazardous climb to the sloping plateau at the summit.

A party from the University of Durham succeeded in landing on the island in July 1980 with Army assistance and stayed there for about a fortnight studying the ecology and wildlife. They occupied an old dwelling which was used by the St Kildans for shelter and which may date from the Iron Age. And not only are the wild descendants of the domestic sheep, abandoned when the St Kildans were evacuated in 1930, still surviving there but, together with the adjacent stacks, this is the nesting site for nearly forty per cent of the entire world population of gannets.

In spite of its exposed situation the skewed summit of Boreray is covered in lush grass and, remarkably, there are at least 130 types of flowering plant including some alpines which probably relish the cool climate and absence of disturbance. There are still traces of lazybeds and one can only marvel at the thought of carrying loads of seaweed up these high cliffs to manure the potatoes! By 1889 sheep had replaced the lazybed culture but even these had to be hoisted up the cliffs.

The most dangerous visit by the St Kildans took place on a night each September. This was to kill the gannets, or *guga* (Gaelic for a young gannet, or a fat silly fellow), when they were asleep. Gannets were important items in the islanders' subsistence culture. Normally about seven men would land, wearing woollen socks to avoid slipping on the slimy rock. The boat would then stand off with a crew of five and drift around all night. Gannets always post a 'sentry' and this bird had to be killed silently first. Then the sleeping birds were quietly clubbed to death or strangled with fowling rods – which sounds easy until one remembers that the gannet is a big bird, ferocious when disturbed, and the rocky ledges are narrow and treacherous in the dark. Some birds would be gutted and left stored in the cleits on Boreray, but several hundred would be loaded aboard the Hirta boat at daybreak. Despite this annual massacre nature kept an equilibrium. Birds still survive here; it is the human beings who have gone.

In April or May the St Kildans visited Boreray to collect sea-bird eggs and count the sheep and in June they returned to collect the wool. Dogs were carried up the cliff to help gather the flock. After several days, the men would cut out an area of turf. This could be seen from Hirta and it was the signal to send a boat – weather, of course, permitting. In earlier times women accompanied the men and while the men tended the sheep the women would catch and kill puffins.

Pointed Stac an Armin, which means the warrior or steward is, at 196 metres (643 feet), the highest monolith in the British Isles; and its companion, Stac Lee, still has an ancient

Boreray, behind Stac an Armin

bothy or shelter on its top, exposed to the Atlantic gales, yet dry inside and able to accommodate two people. When it was climbed by mountaineers in 1969 the south-east corner was considered the best landing point but best is a relative term – even on a calm day the Atlantic swell will move a boat up or down by five metres or more. Apparently the St Kildans lassoed an iron peg when landing. As the boat reached the top of the swell they would jump, find slippery hand and footholds, and start to climb.

We had sailed over from Village Bay on Hirta where we had seen, bobbing at anchor, a tiny blue yacht with an outboard motor. Its owners were a leathery old married couple who told us they sailed their craft everywhere and had crossed the Atlantic in it four times. A nor'-easterly gale was forecast for that evening which would blow straight in to the bay. They said they were leaving immediately for a safe anchorage in Harris and we said we would be not far behind them. Later, on studying the horizon from near Boreray, we could see no sign of them and then to our amazement we spotted them sailing westwards into the wide-open North Atlantic – next landfall, Nova Scotia. We watched with interest as the sail slowly dwindled and disappeared over the horizon. 'Maybe they don't know east from west,' said Craig dryly. 'No wonder they've crossed the Atlantic so many times.'

SCARP

. . . the island Scarp, two miles in circumference. . . is a high land covered with heath and grass. . .

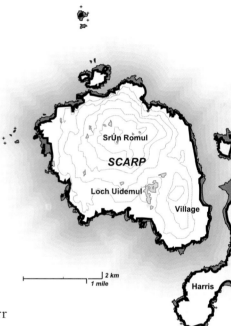

On 14th January 1934, attended by an eighty-five-year-old midwife in her home on Scarp, Mrs Christina Maclennan gave birth to a healthy child but, as the mother was still suffering the next day, it was decided to call the doctor. There was no telephone on Scarp so an islander crossed to Hushinish on Harris where he found the telephone out of order and had to send the postman's son by bus to Tarbert with a message for the doctor. The doctor decided that Mrs Maclennan should really be in hospital. The sea was rough so she had to be tied to a stretcher laid across an open boat and from Hushinish she travelled the seventeen miles of bumpy road to Tarbert on the floor of the bus. From there she was driven by car to Stornoway. At the hospital the cause of her distress was quickly discovered for she gave birth to a second healthy child, and felt much better for it! Thus twins were born on different islands, in different counties and on different dates.

This story, widely reported in the press at the time, came to the ears of an enthusiastic young German engineer who was building his own successful rockets. On 28th July 1934, remembered in the islands as *Latha na Rocait* – the day of the rocket, Herr Gerhard Zucker chose to demonstrate his new method of communication on Scarp – rocket-mail. Special stamps were printed for the occasion and a letter was written to the king. The one-metre-long solid-fuel rocket could carry several thousand letters at 1000mph but when Herr Zucker lit the fuse the rocket exploded scattering mail over a wide area. The local postmaster had the letters collected and stamped with violet ink reading – 'Damaged by first explosion at Scarp – Harris'. A second experiment with the same mail fired from Harris back to Scarp was successful. Even so, the project was abandoned, although a few of the original letters addressed to Orkney eventually reached their destination after travelling by rocket, ferry, car, mail-steamer, railway and Highland Airways.

Scarp is an Old Norse name meaning sharp, stony, mountain terrain which is a good description of this 2500-acre island which rises to over 300 metres in height. In the 1930s geologists discovered that some of the rock was unique for the region as it has an asbestos content.

The island was settled by eight farming families in 1810 and the population increased after clearances on Harris, rising in due course to over 200. That number could not be supported as there is very little cultivable land and no all-weather harbour so many families drifted away. Even in the 1950s the economy was still very basic – potatoes, cabbages, oats, turnips, milk, fish, and some lobster fishing. There was some piped water, one small shop, and a telephone (installed in 1947), but no electricity. The last seven crofters sadly packed their bags in 1971 leaving the village, which is in the south-east corner and partly sheltered from the Atlantic winds by a low hill, to be turned into holiday accommodation.

Scarp is yet another island with an unfortunate recent history of ownership. It was bought by a Panamanian company for £100 in 1978 as a speculation, sold in 1983 for £50,000 to Libco Ltd, then resold almost immediately to Orbitglen Ltd for £500,000. Both these latter deals were by Nazmudin Virani who was a director of BCCI, the bank which put up the money. When BCCI collapsed the property was resold for £155,000.

Although the Kyle of Scarp is a short crossing from Harris, landing at the pier can sometimes be difficult as the very shallow sea exaggerates the swell. But the island itself is unspoilt, with coastal caves and waterfalls, and a delightful walk up the central glen past the mill loch and Loch Uidemul with only skylarks and sheep for company. From the height of Sròn Romul it is possible to see the peaks of St Kilda and, when the weather is kind and the eyes keen, even the Flannan Isles are a small interruption on the vast, empty ocean.

Jandara *in the Kyle of Scarp*

TARANSAY

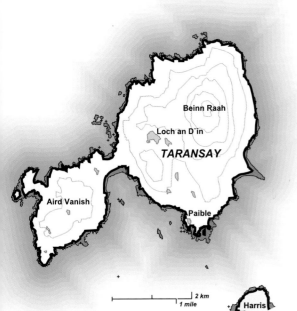

. . . the isle of Taransay. . . yields much yellow talk. It has two chapels, one dedicated to St Tarran, the other to St Keith.

. . . There is an ancient tradition among the natives here, that a man must not be buried in St Tarran's, nor a woman in St Keith's, because otherwise the corpse would be found above ground the day after it is interred. I told them this was a most ridiculous fancy which they might soon perceive by experience if they would put it to a trial. Roderick Campbell, who resides there, resolved to embrace the first opportunity that offered, in order to undeceive the credulous vulgar; and accordingly a poor man in this island, who died a year after, was buried in St Tarran's chapel, contrary to the ancient custom and tradition of this place, but his corpse is still in the grave, from whence it is not like to rise until the general resurrection. This instance has delivered the credulous natives from this unreasonable fancy. . .

. . Every great family in the isles had a chief Druid, who foretold future events, and decided all causes, civil and ecclesiastical. It is reported of them that they wrought in the night time, and rested all day. Caesar says they worshipped a deity under the name of Taramis, or Taran, which in Welsh signifies Thunder; and in the ancient language of the Highlanders, Torin signifies Thunder also. . .

By my reckoning Taransay counts as quite a big island as a lot of walking is required to cover its 3600 acres of rough up-and-down ground. Great slabs of grey gneiss traversed by veins of granite break through the tussocky grass like worn patches on an old rug and the small indigenous herd of red deer make tracks around them.

Nowadays the island is used solely for sheep farming by John Mackay who lives at Horgabost on neighbouring Harris but it was not always so. Back in the 1840s there were sixteen houses accommodating nearly ninety islanders and even in 1911 seventy-six inhabitants still lived a tough but rewarding life here. Then two world wars gave the islanders a glimpse of another way of life and the population slowly drained away. By 1942 Taransay had been abandoned and, although a few returned for a spell, by 1974 they had moved back to the Harris 'mainland' and the sheep and deer had the island to themselves.

On the beach, Taransay

This is Taran's isle but Taran is an uncertain figure in Celtic history. According to Adomnan he was the son of a noble Pictish family who requested St Columba's protection. Columba agreed and asked Feradach, a rich man on Islay, to accept him in his retinue and treat him as a friend but in due course Feradach had him murdered. Columba was naturally outraged and demanded divine judgement. Another possibility was the Irish saint Ternan or Torannan who had a great influence on the Pictish mainland but no known connection with the islands. However, as one of the chapels on Taransay was dedicated to a St Taran he seems a more likely candidate.

Taransay is divided in two by a low sandy neck of dunes. The village of Paible on the larger part of the island was the main settlement. Beinn Raah, 267 metres high, dominates this area with a ridge to the north and lesser peaks to the south-west where there are a number of small lochs. The Mill Burn – Allt a' Mhuilinn – joins the sea at Paible and tracing its course makes an interesting walk up past Loch Cromlach and Loch Shinnadale to its source at Loch an Duinn. Here there is a small fort or dun on an islet near the east shore – an islet which is probably man-made – a crannog. A further slog up to the top of Beinn Raah provides a stunning view of the mountains of Harris sweeping round to the lone peak at Toe Head. A hillside bothy provides useful emergency accommodation for visitors. There is a house at Paible which is maintained by the owner and used exclusively for accommodation by the farm workers during regular visits to tend the sheep. They usually stay for ten days or so at a time. Otherwise the houses, and the schoolhouse which closed in 1935, are in ruins.

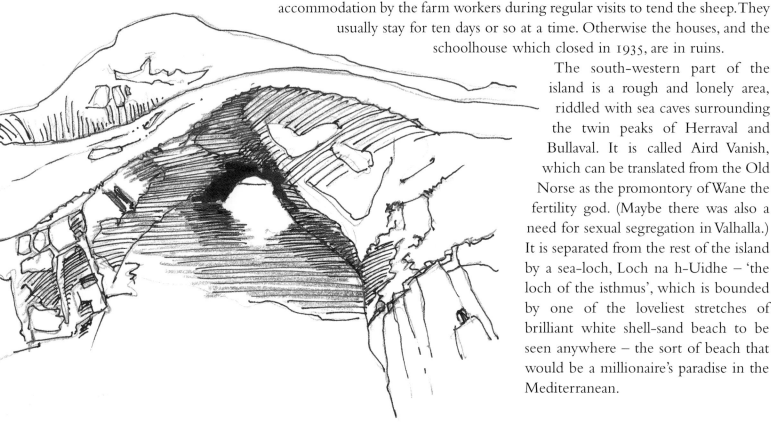

The south-western part of the island is a rough and lonely area, riddled with sea caves surrounding the twin peaks of Herraval and Bullaval. It is called Aird Vanish, which can be translated from the Old Norse as the promontory of Wane the fertility god. (Maybe there was also a need for sexual segregation in Valhalla.) It is separated from the rest of the island by a sea-loch, Loch na h-Uidhe – 'the loch of the isthmus', which is bounded by one of the loveliest stretches of brilliant white shell-sand beach to be seen anywhere – the sort of beach that would be a millionaire's paradise in the Mediterranean.

BERNERAY

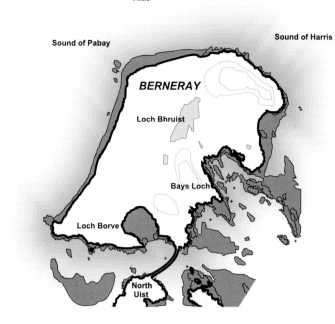

. . . Sir Norman Macleod, who has his residence in the isle of Bernera, went to the isle of Skye about business, without appointing any time for his return; his servants, in his absence, being all together in the large hall at night, one of them who had been accustomed to see the second-sight told the rest they must remove, for they would have abundance of other company in the hall that night. One of his fellow-servants answered that there was very little appearance of that. . . They continued to argue the improbability of it, because of the darkness of the night, and the danger of coming through the rocks that lie round the isle; but within an hour after, one of Sir Norman's men came to the house, bidding them provide lights, etc., for his master had newly landed; and thus the prediction was immediately accomplished.

. . . Sir Norman hearing of it called for the seer, and examined him about it; he answered that he had seen the spirit called Browny in human shape... carrying an old woman that sat by the fire to the door. . . by neck and heels, which made him laugh heartily, and gave occasion to the rest to conclude he was mad to laugh so without reason. This instance was told me by Sir Norman himself. . .

'Chust keep close past the peacons and when the ruin meets the end of Mary's garden wall turn to the orange puoy. Go close to it. (Oh! but not too close, mind!) After that it will be plain sailing – nothing to pother about till you hit the other side.' So said Big John, better known as Iain Mór.

It is only recently that directions have been published on how to avoid the rocks and reefs of shallow Bays Loch when trying to reach Berneray's harbour. The locals navigate entirely by instinct. We had radioed Angus for information, but he was out lobster-fishing and his radio was not working, so Big John, bless him, had offered to help. We thanked him, signed off, heaved a sigh, and turned *Jandara* towards the beacons. We had been told that one old islander, bringing a visitor across from Harris, ran his boat onto a rock. 'But I thought you knew all the rocks!' cried the visitor. 'Aye,' said the old man, 'I do. And that is one of them.'

We had no idea which garden wall belonged to Mary but we arrived safely nevertheless – more by good luck than navigation – and tucked ourselves into Berneray's secure but tiny

Sea and sand in the Sound of Harris

harbour. Big John's enormous bulk came aboard later and Ian offered him a whisky by way of thanks for his instructions. He had already consumed a fair quantity and was feeling particularly upset because a small English yacht, locked up and deserted, was obstructing the ferry-berth and she was – heaven forbid – flying the Cross of St George as her ensign. 'All my years in the Merchant Naify I have nefer, efer, seen such a thing,' bellowed Big John crashing his fist down on the extended leaf of our saloon table. I quickly edged my knee under the leaf to try to support it. 'Do they not know that it's the red tuster should be flying on a Pritish ship?' A great ham of a fist hit the table again and I winced with pain.

When the whisky bottle was empty, Big John suggested that we all go and see Angus. I declined as my kneecap was shattered. 'But I'll trive you there. . .' he said.

Looking at Big John reminded me that Berneray was the birthplace of the 'Cape Breton Giant' – one of the world's tallest and strongest men. Angus MacAskill was a well-proportioned 2.36 metres (7 feet 9 inches) in height and weighed 425 pounds. He died in Canada in 1863, when he was only thirty-eight years old.

I felt it was important to write about the lovely isle of Berneray because it recently lost its status as a separate island. A great sweep of causeway now stretches out from North Uist welding the two islands into one and with its completion Berneray – all of its 2500 acres and population of about 140 – will never be quite the same again. For example, the island still has large stretches of unspoilt machair, supporting about 200 different species of wildflower, whereas on the Uists much of this is being ripped apart by rabbits. So an official 'rabbit-free zone' has been created at the causeway and we know what that means – but will the rabbits?

All the machair on Berneray is on the west side, together with rough grazing, a great line of sand dunes, and a stunning stretch of white shell-sand beach – about four kilometres of perfection. A wide freshwater loch, Loch Bruist, is almost at the centre of the island, while two low hills and all the housing are on the east side. It is here that the harbour, built with EC funds in the late 1980s, tucks into the side of reef-ridden Bays Loch.

Berneray's light shell-sandy soil, which is still manured with kelp, grows a generous and tasty crop of potatoes and for many years most of the potatoes eaten on Harris were imported from here. Nowadays, sheep farming and fishing for prawns, lobsters and velvet crabs are the main industries. Trim new suburban bungalows, however incongruous in such a beautiful setting, are appearing among the deserted black houses and this is a good example of how years of decline have been replaced by hope and a belief in a viable future.

Berneray's greatest asset, of course, is its friendly inhabitants who always make a stranger feel welcome. This was highlighted in the late 1980s when the Prince of Wales chose Berneray as the island on which to 'get away from it all'. It says much for Hebridean loyalty and respect for privacy that not a single man, woman or child breathed a word about their famous guest to the media. It was the Prince himself who revealed the facts four years later.

THE
SHIANTS

. . . There are three small islands here; the two southern islands are separated only by spring-tides. . . Island-More hath a chapel in it dedicated to the Virgin Mary, and is fruitful in corn and grass; the island joining to it on the west is only for pasturage. . . I saw a couple of eagles here:. . . those eagles are so careful of the place of their abode, that they never yet killed any sheep or lamb in the island, though the bones of lambs, of fawns, and wild-fowls, are frequently found in and about their nests; so they make their purchase in the opposite islands, the nearest of which is a league distant. . .

. . . This island is very strong and inaccessible, save on one side where the ascent is narrow, and somewhat resembling a stair, but a great deal more high and steep; notwithstanding which the cows pass and repass by it safely, though one would think it uneasy for a man to climb. . .

. . . The cows here are much fatter than any I saw in the Island of Lewis. . .

Some say that the ghostly and menacing Blue Men of the Minch who live in the Enchanted Sound by the Shiant Islands are storm kelpies who must be treated with great respect by sailors. Others say they are bad-tempered angels who fell into the sea when they were expelled from Heaven. A century ago the Rev John Campbell, minister of Tiree, claimed that one of them followed his boat – 'a blue-covered man, with a long, grey face, and floating from the waist out of the water.' The creature sometimes came so close that he could have touched him. One skipper claimed that he had to answer a Blue Man's questions in rhyming Gaelic couplets on the threat of being dragged beneath the Minch if his replies were not sufficiently poetic. No wonder the Shiants (pron. *shunts*) are the enchanted isles (*na h-eileanan seunta* in Gaelic).

The group, which is north of Skye, is made up of three main islands. Eilean Mhuire, or Mary's island, has steep cliffs on all sides and difficult access but its high plateau is covered with fertile arable land and ancient lazybeds, a tiny freshwater lochan, and the remains of dwellings marked by clumps of nettles. Its ruined chapel was still in use at the time of the Reformation and was dedicated to the Virgin Mary. Eilean Mhuire lies a short distance to the east of Garbh Eilean, so that the group almost forms a bay with a south-eastern exposure.

Opposite: The lone cottage on Eilean an Tigh

Garbh Eilean ('rough island') is connected with Eilean an Tigh ('house island') by a low narrow neck of rubble and shingle and I therefore count them as one island of 350 acres. The sea covers the isthmus at spring tides and during storms. Eilean an Tigh has precipitous cliffs on its eastern side but Garbh Eilean – the back-street Manhattan of the Western Isles – towers above it. The spectacular cliffs on its north face are a vast city of seabirds, kittiwakes, guillemots, razorbills and fulmars, noisy and rank-smelling. These cliffs are composed of great columnar basalt skyscrapers almost two metres in diameter and well over 120 metres in height. Compare this with the well-known basalt pillars of Fingal's Cave on Staffa which are a mere ten metres high.

There is a lone cottage on the west side of Eilean an Tigh, near the shingle link with Eilean Garbh and close to a crystal clear spring of fresh water hidden by lush green grass and wild flowers. When Sir Compton MacKenzie bought the islands in 1925 he renovated the cottage and stayed there during the summer months when he wanted solitude for writing. In 1937 he sold the islands to the publisher Nigel Nicolson for £1500, and the Nicolson family still owns them. The grazing rights are let to a sheep farmer on Scalpay who keeps the cottage repaired and uses it during visits to tend the sheep.

Behind the cottage is the ruin of an older dwelling and on the north side there are the remains of two more. These once housed five families but by 1796 only one shepherd and his family were resident and then they met with tragedy – his wife and son fell to their death while collecting sheep above the steep cliffs. Not long after, his daughter fell to her death while collecting sea-birds' eggs leaving only the shepherd and his younger daughter. Then he also died – but of natural causes or possibly heartbreak – leaving his daughter alone on the island. Ten days went by before the weather was settled enough for her to row the twelve miles to Harris and she never returned. (This sad tale loses some of its drama when we learn that she had quite often rowed over to Harris to visit her boyfriend.)

The islands are rat-infested, probably from a shipwreck, and Sir Compton Mackenzie rashly imported cats to try to deal with them (cats are a menace on any island). However the cats died, or were killed by the rats which are large and fearless! Because rats steal the eggs and young of sea birds there was a recent proposal for controlled eradication by poisoning. Then it was pointed out that these are not common Brown Rats, *Rattus novergicus*, but Black Rats, *Rattus rattus*, the plague rats of old. They are very rare in the British Isles, so despite being puffin predators – and puffins being a 'protected' species – the rats are also now 'protected'!

ISAY

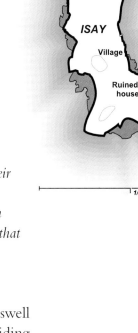

. . .On the west side of Vaterness promontory, within the mouth of Loch-Fallart, lies Isa, two miles in compass, being fruitful in corn and grass, and is commodious for fishing of cod and ling. . .

. . .The fishers and others told me that there is a big herring almost double the size of any of its kind, which leads all that are in a bay, and the shoal follows it wherever it goes. This leader is by the fishers called the king of herring, and when they chance to catch it alive, they drop it carefully into the sea; for they judge it petty treason to destroy a fish of that name. . .

. . .The natives preserve and dry their herring without salt, for the space of eight months, provided they be taken after the tenth of September, they use no other art in it but take out their guts, and then tying a rush about their necks, hang them by pairs upon a rope made of heath cross a house; and they eat well, and free from putrefaction, after eight months keeping in this manner. Cod, ling, herring, mackeral, haddock, whiting, turbot, together with all other fish that are in the Scots seas, abound. . .

'There is a beautiful little island in the Loch of Dunvegan, called Isa,' recalled Boswell in 1773. 'M'Leod said he would give it to Dr Johnson, on condition of his residing on it three months in the year; nay one month. Dr Johnson was highly amused with the fancy. I have seen him please himself with little things, even with mere ideas like the present. He talked a great deal of this island; – how he would build a house there, – how he would fortify it, – how he would have cannon, – how he would plant, – how he would sally out and take the isle of Muck; – and then he laughed with uncommon glee, and could hardly leave off. . . M'Leod encouraged the fancy of Dr Johnson's becoming owner of an island; told him that it was the practice in this country to name every man by his lands; and begged leave to drink to him in that mode: "Island Isa, your health!"'

Grass-covered Isay with its two small companions, Mingay and Clett, lies peacefully in Loch Dunvegan. The name Isay (pron. *eee*-sha) probably comes from the Old Norse meaning 'porpoise island'. In the early 1800s Isay's 148 acres supported an industrious population of about ninety people. It was a big fishing station with its own general store until the Salt Tax spoiled the fishing industry. The last twelve crofter families were cleared for sheep in 1860. Today, a line of more than eighteen ruined cottages and black houses runs along the east shore towards the remnants of a crude stone jetty. At the south end of this village is the ruined main house which in Dr Johnson's time was probably quite an attractive residence in spite of its gruesome history. Its west gable now has a large 'arched' hole through it giving it the appearance of the west gable of a church. This is evidently where the fireplace for the main hall on the first floor used to be. The main entrance to this hall is from the higher ground level on the south side by way of a stone staircase. The ground floor appears to have been divided into three rooms and there is an outhouse on the east gable – possibly the kitchen.

The story of the house goes back to the early 16th century when Roderick MacLeod of Lewis owned the island. He wanted his grandson to inherit the island of Raasay and the lands of Gairloch but there were two entire families of his relatives with a first claim to the estates and they would obviously have to be eliminated. He therefore invited both families to a banquet on Isay promising that they would learn something which would be to their advantage. They all turned up and during the meal Roderick made a brief speech saying that he wished to have the private and personal opinion of everyone present on a matter 'of great importance'. He left the room. Each guest was then summoned in turn and escorted to a room where Roderick had him, or her, quietly slaughtered. His grandson gained his inheritance.

Summer boat excursions which leave from near Dunvegan Castle sometimes stop at Isay to allow visitors to explore the island. For those visiting the island in their own boat at high water it is important to remember that the hidden reef which continues northwards from the island is a long one and it is very easy to misjudge its length. So if the skipper of the tourist boat waves at you, don't just wave back as you sail happily on – he may be trying to tell you something 'of great importance'.

Scene of a massacre

The shark-oil factory in Acarsaid, Soa

SOAY

. . . there is an anchoring place for barks, between Skye and the isle Soa. . .

There are several Scottish islands called Soay, or Soa, which means 'sheep island' in Old Norse. In this case I am referring to the one near Skye which was very lightly populated until the clearances on Skye in the mid-1800s when over 100 dispossessed crofters chose to settle on it rather than go to America.

Soay's 2500 acres were the property of the MacLeods of Dunvegan from the 13th century until 1946, just after World War II, when Gavin Maxwell bought it for a shark-fishing venture. There was still a small resident population, one of whom was Joseph 'Tex' Geddes who held the crofting rights to twenty-one of the twenty-five island crofts and who was Maxwell's harpooner. An old fishing industry house became the 'factory' and a brick and corrugated asbestos shed, water storage tank and large boiler were added. Shark liver oil was in great demand by the pharmaceutical industry at the time and docile basking sharks were easy prey but it was because so many of these inoffensive creatures were slaughtered that they are now rarely seen in West Coast waters. By 1949 synthetic substitutes had been found and there was an immediate drop in the value of shark oil which brought the venture to an end. Maxwell then wrote a book about his experiences titled *Harpoon at a Venture*. Of course he later became much better known for his wonderful book about otters, *Ring of Bright Water*, which gained him world recognition as a 'conservationist'.

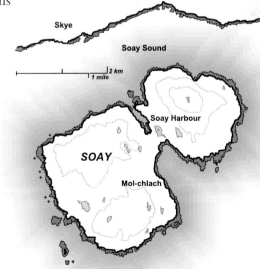

One unfortunate consequence of the end of shark hunting was a loss of employment for the Soay islanders and in 1952 they petitioned the government for evacuation. Eventually the government agreed and on 20th June 1953 with a great deal of publicity and a lone piper playing a lament the SS *Hebrides* evacuated the crofters and took them to Craignure on Mull where land had been purchased for them by the government. The affair had some overtones of the sad evacuation of St Kilda in 1930.

Only one family refused to be evacuated – that of Mr 'Tex' Geddes – and forty years later he achieved his ambition and became the sole owner and laird of Soay. In recent years the island has seen a small increase in population although this is partly from holiday homes. Mail and stores are landed on a regular monthly basis and there is irregular contact with Elgol on Skye and Mallaig on the mainland.

Soay is dwarfed by the Cuillin mountains which tower up on the opposite shore of the narrow sound. It is a dumb-bell shaped island with a narrow gut almost cutting it in half and forming the anchorage, Acarsaid Soa, on one side of the central isthmus. A profusion of deciduous bushes and trees such as birch, oak, and rowan cover this low saddle attracting a variety of birdlife including nesting herons and ravens which cross over the sound from Skye.

The harbour today has a charming deserted aspect and the old shark-oil factory buildings now form an interesting group of derelict structures. Blackbirds nest in the broken, rust-covered boiler stoke-hole and the original two-storey house has only half its slated roof remaining. When it was first constructed in 1849 to help the fishing industry it had curing facilities at ground floor level and accommodation for visiting fishermen upstairs. But at least Maxwell's corrugated-asbestos-roofed shed is still in use as a store for fishing gear. A dry 'mill lade' runs from the storage tank to an 'oven' by the house and the area is littered with the brass cases of rifle cartridges which I can only presume were used to scare the herring gulls away.

There is no pier or jetty, but a cobbled pathway, which was constructed in the early 1900s with government funding, leads from the harbour through the woodland in the central cleft and on past the solar 'telephone exchange'. This was the first of its kind in the world and powers nine telephones for the small settlement of houses facing the southern bay.

THE
CROWLINS

CROWLIN ISLES

...Within less than a mile further is the narrow sound called the Kyle, in order to pass which it is absolutely necessary to have the tide of flood for such as are northward bound, else they will be obliged to retire in disorder, because of the violence of the current; for no wind is able to carry a vessel against it. The quite contrary course is to be observed by vessels coming from the north... there are two rocks in the passage through the Kyle; they are on the castle side, and may be avoided by keeping the middle of the channel...

Sail through Kyleakin, the channel named after old King Haakon and now crossed by the long sweeping curve of the Skye Bridge, and up the Inner Sound between Skye and the mainland and you find a very varied assortment of islands. Flat and fertile Pabay, mountainous Scalpay, tiny Longay, the long stretch of Raasay and Rona, and straight ahead the pink sandstone mound of the Crowlins. At low water this is one island (and I count it as such), but as the tide rises and covers the bladder-wrack and dulse-draped rocks it divides into three – accurately if unimaginatively named in Gaelic 'big island', 'middle island' and 'little island'. Several centuries ago all the smaller islands in the Inner Sound were inhabited by pirates and cut-throats who probably paid 'protection money' to the local chief, MacLeod of Raasay, although that was never officially admitted. At that time the islands were thickly wooded and gave excellent cover, and only 'foreign' ships were attacked – Dutch, Flemish, English and Lowland Scots.

The Crowlins lay in a key position for these nefarious activities and had a useful harbour even if it was not as well-concealed as the magnificent Acairseid Mhór on Rona. Small boats can easily enter the narrow central channel which is secure in almost any weather, but for larger boats access is a bit like threading a needle and the name Crowlin probably comes from the Gaelic *crò linne* for 'eye-of-a-needle channel'. After the age of piracy, and when no longer protected by tree-cover, the population supported themselves mainly by fishing. Forty people were living on these 600 acres in 1841. They had a scattered settlement with a small church in the bay below the lochan but everyone had left by the turn of the century.

This is a group of three well-worn chunks of Torridonian sandstone with volcanic rock intrusions. The coastline is eroded and there are many small caves, and a larger one on the

Anchored in the eye of the needle

east coast beside the ruined settlement. One rock shelter by the anchorage is still used occasionally by local fishermen.

We've often dropped anchor in the Crowlins and I can only think of one occasion when it was dreich and drizzly. Usually the lovely soft colours of the sandstone blend with the evening sky and only an occasional sea bird or the splash of a seal disturb the stillness. Common seals seem to be particularly fond of the north point – Eilean Beag – where there is a small light beacon. A leisurely stroll through the bracken and up the only hill – a mere 114 metres (370 feet) – provides a view across all three island sections. The central lochan on Eilean Mór – Tombstone Loch – reflects the sky and the rounded silhouette of the Red Cuillin and the serrated forms of the Black Cuillin provide a dramatic barrier across the western horizon.

On the one occasion when we anchored in miserable weather we were actually travelling south and heading for Loch Alsh. As we passed the Crowlins we saw through the gloom what looked like a peculiar rock formation. We turned to investigate and found that the 'rock formation' was a yacht high and dry on the shore at the entrance to the harbour. The family were all safely ashore and the hired yacht was luckily undamaged. Apparently the helmsman had cut the corner on leaving the harbour on a falling tide, the keel had stuck in a pebble patch, and the poor thing had slowly settled on her side as the tide ran out. She had been there for a number of hours and the skipper, for reasons best known to himself, had decided not to inform the coastguard. We hung around until she even-tually refloated and sailed on her way and then spent a wet night snug below with some good wine for company.

RAASAY

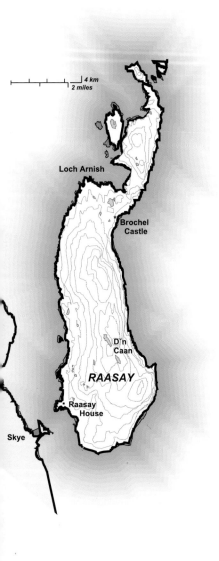

. . . the isle Raasay. . . has some wood on all the quarters of it, the whole is fitter for pasturage than cultivation, the ground being generally very unequal, but very well watered with rivulets and springs. . .

. . . There are some forts in this isle, the highest is in the south end; it is a natural strength, and in form like the crown of a hat; it is called Dun-Cann, which the natives will needs have to be from one Canne, cousin to the king of Denmark. The other lies on the side, is an artificial fort, three stories high, and is called Castle Vreokle...

. . . The proprietor of the isle is Mr MacLeod, a cadet of the family of that name; his seat is in the village Clachan. The inhabitants have as great veneration for him as any subjects can have for their king. They preserve the memory of the deceased ladies of the place by erecting a little pyramid of stone for each of them, with the lady's name. These pyramids are by them called crosses; several of them are built of stone and lime, and have three steps of gradual ascent to them. There are eight such crosses about the village, which is adorned with a little tower, and lesser houses, and an orchard with several sorts of berries, pot herbs, &c. The inhabitants are all Protestants. . .

We slipped into the bay beside the Raasay Narrows and picked up a mooring for a short break while we ate our midday piece. Stone mermaids with unbelievable busts decorate the 'Battery' on the island shore and Raasay House stands well back among the sheltering trees. It is run as an Outdoor Centre and we had read that visiting yachts were welcome.

Half-an-hour later we were surprised to find the busty mermaids almost in our cockpit. We should have felt honoured but we had, of course, committed an unforgivable act of bad-seamanship by picking up a large mooring buoy on the assumption that it was part of a substantial mooring. Luckily, the error was spotted before we ran aground and we were able to drag the mooring back to its original position and use our anchor instead. (I can remember another buoy we once found attached to nothing more than a rusty hammer.) Later, when we apologised to the young Adonis in charge of the Outdoor Centre he grinned and explained that the mooring was for dinghies.

Raasay House is a fine example of how history and circumstances can ruin an island property. With a perfect outlook across the sound to the mountains of Skye this was the

Raasay House – where Dr Johnson stayed

family seat of the MacLeods of Raasay. The MacLeods were Protestants but chose actively to support the Jacobites – it would seem mainly for sheer bloody-mindedness – by sending 100 men and 26 pipers to Culloden in 1746. They then compounded their error by hiding the Young Pretender in a shepherd's hut on the island. In reprisal Government troops burned down their home and nearly every house on the island, destroyed the boats, murdered the men, raped the women and 'there was not left in the whole island a four-footed beast, hen or chicken.'

A few years later the MacLeods stubbornly rebuilt Raasay House (although the Regency frontage wasn't added until the early 1800s) and it was here that they lavishly entertained Boswell and Johnson in 1773. But thirty years later poverty was widespread and islanders began to emigrate. The Laird, John MacLeod, tried to help but by 1843 he was so deeply in debt that he had to sell the island. The evictions which followed have been immortalised in haunting verse by Raasay's world-renowned Gaelic poet, Sorley MacLean.

Eighty years passed before the Government stepped in and bought the island (in 1922) for £37,000. In the 1960s it tried to recoup some of this modest cost by selling Raasay House and other key properties to a Sussex pathologist. He visited the island once and never returned, but refused to sell. Years of acrimony, deterioration and Government inaction followed during which vandals stripped Raasay House completely and destroyed its valuable library. Then in 1979 the doctor was at last persuaded to sell the properties to the Highland and Islands Development Board for a high price.

Raasay is remarkably beautiful and it is sheltered from the worst of the weather by Skye. The name means 'roe-deer island' in Old Norse but it is red deer that are dominant today although animal life also includes alpine hare, pine marten, otter, water shrew and a unique sub-species of bank vole.

A road runs the length of the island from the ferry terminal, through the main village of Inverarish which is set in pleasant woodland, to Brochel Castle, the pirate stronghold of the MacLeods in the 15th century. On the way it passes Raasay's highest peak – Dùn Caan – which looks like a truncated Fujiama. It is 443 metres high yet the pudgy and irrepressible James Boswell climbed it and danced a reel on the flat top 'in sheer exuberance'.

The road running north from Brochel to Arnish was built single-handedly by Calum MacLeod, a postman and another thrawn MacLeod clansman, because the council refused to help. He started in 1966 but died soon after completing the monumental task in 1988.

RONA

. . . This little isle is the most unequal rocky piece of ground to be seen anywhere: there is but very few acres fit for digging, the whole is covered with long heath, erica-baccifera, mertillus, and some mixture of grass; it is reckoned very fruitful in pasturage: most of the rocks consist of the hectic stone, and a considerable part of them is of a red colour.

. . . There is a bay on the south-west end of the isle, with two entries, the one is on the west side, the other on the south, but the latter is only accessible; it has a rock within the entry, and a good fishing. . .

'Quite repulsive' claimed the *Gazateer* in 1844, yet I consider South Rona to be one of our loveliest islands. Such is the changing perception of beauty.

This was Pirate HQ for the Inner Sound in the 16th century and it would be hard to discover a safer hideout. Approaching Rona's rocky west coast the spacious natural harbour once known as the Pirates' Port is almost entirely hidden from view. It is now merely called Acairseid Mhór – Big Harbour – and an arrow is painted on the rockface to help yachtsmen find the entrance. Even so there is the weird impression of sailing straight into a cliff-face until the harbour suddenly opens up with its defensive inner barrier of underwater rocks. MacLeod of Raasay collected 'protection money' from the pirates and turned a blind eye on their misdemeanours. So, like that other island chieftain, MacNeil of Barra, who carried out piracy on a much bigger scale, MacLeod prospered.

Ian, Craig and I first visited Rona many years ago on *Jeananne*. The island had been uninhabited for decades but the single lonely house overlooking the harbour – the 'widow's house', as we called it – had an unlocked door, unbroken windows, box bed, Welsh dresser, and a leather kist by the fireside.

I have been drawn back many times since then to this wild and wonderful place. Although the harbour is now popular, the island never loses its desolate charm. Apart from a patch of native woodland, its 2000 acres are so barren, tussocky, boggy, rock-strewn, and up-and-down that it is easy to lose both one's sense of direction and sense of reality. How this island supported nearly 200 people in the 19th century is a miracle but the deserted village complete with schoolhouse and church still stands at Acairseid Thioram – Dry Harbour. Some houses were occupied until the 1930s. On subsequent visits we have sadly seen the 'widow's house' (Rona Lodge) deteriorate as day-trippers took their savage toll until, a few years ago, the new Danish owner tastefully restored it to its traditional state.

The reason why we called it the 'widow's house' was from a tragic tale which we had heard but which I have only recently been able to correct and verify. The actual 'widow's house' it turns out was, in fact, a small ruined bothy by the jetty – now repaired and used for storage. In 1840 it was occupied by the Mackenzie family, the only residents at Big Harbour at the time. That summer there was a severe drought and Kenneth Mackenzie sailed over to Portree to fetch a supply of fresh water. On the return trip he was lost at sea but his widow Janet could not believe that her husband had drowned so every night she kept a light burning in the cottage window to guide his boat back into harbour. Janet brought up her children and kept the light burning for twelve long years, but in 1852 she gave up and emigrated to Australia with her three sons.

This explains a mishap we had when leaving the island on that first visit so many years ago. The directions in use at the time gave the cottage window as a leading mark for avoiding a rock. The cottage referred to, however, was the widow's house by the jetty which had long since fallen into ruin and, to us, the only recognisable cottage was Rona Lodge. As it was low water when we entered the harbour the rocks were visible so there was no problem. Leaving was a different matter. It was approaching high water, Ian was on the helm, and I had carefully taken a bearing on the 'cottage' window. Craig, seeing that the ship was in such competent hands, went below to visit the head which was situated over *Jeananne's* starboard bilge keel. A few minutes later it was the starboard keel that struck the rock and I will never forget the look on Craig's face as, pants round his ankles, he shot out of the head like a cork from a bottle. New sailing instructions, which did not rely on cottage windows, were issued a year or two later but it is only now that I have discovered the truth!

Before the island church was built in 1912 the islanders worshipped in a cave and even in later years it was still a tradition to have babies baptised there. I wanted to see 'Church Cave' but there was no reference to it on any map. I wandered over great tracts of the island without success then on one occasion thought I had spotted it from *Jandara* and struggled for hours to reach the marked position but ended up on the wrong side of a precipitous cleft. Then in the evening, returning discouraged to the boat, a workman who was renovating the Lodge gave us directions on how to reach it.

The cave is like a flattened Gothic vault and there is a low stone pillar for a pulpit and flat slab for an altar. Near it is the font – a depression in a stone fed by drips of water from the cave roof. Rows of stones are laid out as pews for the congregation.

Sitting on a 'pew' high above the sea, surrounded by the ghosts of islanders and with the Inner Sound, the Torridon mountains, and great banks of cumulous clouds as a backdrop to the altar, I realised that this magnificent setting would surely turn the most mediocre of sermons into a masterpiece.

The Pirates' Port on Rona

Stac Pollaidh behind Eilean Fada

TANERA BEG

. . .There is abundance of white and red coral. . . It grows on the rocks, and is frequently interwoven with the roots of the alga. The red seems to be a good fresh colour when first taken out of the sea, but in a few hours after it becomes pale. Some of the natives take a quantity of the red coral, adding the yolk of an egg roasted to it, for the diarrhoea. Both the red and white coral here is not above five inches long, and about the bigness of a goose quill.

When the weather is wet, windy and generally unpleasant a sheltered anchorage has the same appeal as a warm room on a winter's night. How pleasant to cross the threshold and leave the disturbed sea and noisy wind outside – like closing the door and drawing the curtains.

Our discovery of the anchorage at Tanera Beg was not like that; at least, not when we arrived. We had run up from Loch Ewe to the Summer Isles, whisked along by a brisk southerly from one patch of cloud shadow to the next. We skirted Priest Island, rounded Eilean Dubh, and slipped in to the 'Cabbage Patch' on Tanera Mór – a one-time favourite anchorage between two tiny islets. But it was cluttered with moorings and we didn't relish spending the night beside the fields of fish-farm cages which filled the bay. So we carried on round the north end (which is aptly called 'the back of the bed-board' in Gaelic) and tiptoed through the adjoining islets and skerries. Harry, Brenda and Ronald were aboard and Ronald had been this way before so he was able to guide us through with confidence and into the delightful anchorage between Tanera Beg and Eilean Fada Mór.

As soon as the wind was blanketed by the hill, the only sounds were the distant crash of breakers, far away on the other side of the island, and the piping of an oyster-catcher objecting to our intrusion. We decided to postpone a visit ashore till the following morning and after a meal lazily took our drinks into the cockpit. The sunset was spectacular. The whole world was suffused with pink which brought out subtle shades in the rose-coloured Torridonian sandstone around us. The sea picked up all the reflections and these were only disturbed when a family of eider ducks

119

paddled past. Then, as it grew darker, the great mass of Stac Pollaidh towering behind Eilean Fada caught the low rays of the sun and an otter slipped into the water cutting a wake along the shoreline. These are the unforgettable moments when there can be no better place in the world!

On the following morning, when the tide went out, we were greeted by the sight of beautiful displays of coral on the shores of both Tanera Beg and Eilean Fada Mór with a great bank of pink coral sand lying between. In 1938 the naturalist, Frank Fraser Darling, settled on neighbouring Tanera Mór and stayed there until 1944. It was uninhabited at the time and apart from studying the plants and wildlife he also farmed part of the land and recorded his experiences in a book called *Island Farm*. The soil in the largest field – known as Big Park – was of poor quality so he set about turning it into productive arable land by following the well-known principles of Highland and Island lazybed crofting using readily-obtained materials as fertilisers. Seaweed (mixed with some boiler slag) provided the potash content, and clover provided the nitrogen, but he had a problem finding lime – which is traditionally supplied by shell-sand – as Tanera Mór has no shell-sand beaches. His problem was solved when he discovered the bank of beautiful coral sand on Tanera Beg and he would sail across at low water and collect it by the boatload to fertilise the field. I am relieved that he had no modern mechanical devices to help him or we may not have had the beauty of that sand-bank to admire today.

Tanera Beg's 160 acres are enclosed within a very irregular coastline broken by small pebble coves sheltered between low cliffs and overhung by green terraces of honeysuckle and dwarf willow. Beneath the summit of the central hill is a tiny lochan – really no more than a large pool – and from there the heather-clad slope runs over a bluff. Here a shallow valley crosses the island with the trace of a raised beach in it.

The weather was steadily deteriorating and by early afternoon the glories of the previous evening were already a distant memory. We had, in any case, a schedule to keep so we slipped into the kyle between the two Taneras and out into the open sea. We were immediately hit by the fury of gale force winds, lashing rain and great green waves crashing over the bow and breaking across the deck.

We had drawn back the curtains and opened the door.

HANDA

. . .The sea in time of a calm is observed to have a rising motion before the north wind blows, which it has not before the approaching of any other wind.

Women observe that their breasts contract to a lesser bulk when the wind blows from the north, and that then they yield less milk than when it blows from any other quarter. . .

They observe that when the sea yields a kind of pleasant and sweet scent it is a sure presage of fair weather to ensue. . .

It was the potato blight of 1848 which cleared the islanders off Handa; not a wicked landlord with a hunger for mutton. In early times this great tilted outcrop of pink Torridonian sandstone had been used as a burial ground by people on the mainland so that wolves would be unable to scavenge the corpses. Later, seven families settled and started cultivating the rough pastureland. The community thrived, living on a staple diet of oats, potatoes, fish and sea birds. Like St Kilda they had their own 'queen' – the oldest widow – and the men held a daily parliament to decide the allocation of work. The population increased to sixty-five living in a settlement of eleven houses: and then the famine struck, and the whole population emigrated to America. Since then, Handa has been uninhabited, but the old cottages and lazy-beds can still be seen.

Nowadays the island is renowned for its birdlife and is listed as a Site of Special Scientific Interest. In 1961 the public-spirited owners, Major and Dr Jean Balfour of Scourie Estate, leased it to the Royal Society for the Protection of Birds so that it could be maintained as a nature reserve. This arrangement lasted until 1991 when Dr Balfour, who is a former chairman of the Countryside Commission for Scotland and a founder member of the Scottish Wildlife Trust, felt that it was appropriate that the Trust, as a solely Scottish conservation body, should take control.

Apart from birdlife Handa is also noted for its dramatic topography. The precipitous north and west sides rear abruptly out of the sea to a height of over 100 metres. Here the cliffs are dark-red and brown with the horizontal strata sharply outlined in white by sea-bird droppings. In the north-west, and close to the cliffs, is the Big Hill of the Fairies, Sithean Mór. From the top of this hill it is almost possible to see Cape Wrath. The tall

thin figure of the Old Man of Stoer stands out on the far point of Edddrachillis Bay. Directly north of Sithean Mór the cliffs form an amphitheatre, Am Bonair, with a natural arch: and it is on the east side of this bluff, in an inlet or 'geo', that the Great Stack stands – a gigantic rock 115 metres high balanced on three legs and separated from the island by a gap which is only 24 metres wide.

This terrifying narrow chasm has a sheer drop down the wet sandstone face to turbulent ocean surf pounding the rocks far below and it is almost impossible to look across it without feeling at least a tremor of vertigo. Nevertheless, in 1876 Donald MacDonald of Lewis made the first recorded crossing from the clifftop on Handa to the flat top of the Stack by swinging hand-over-hand from a rope. This original crossing was re-enacted by Dr Tom Patey of Ullapool in 1967, except that the traverse was made on that occasion by using a 180-metre nylon rope stretching from one side of the geo to the other and crossing over the Stack. 'It was a thought-provoking experience,' he said afterwards.

Close east of the Great Stack is another stack, Stachan Geodh Bhrisidh – the stack in the broken chasm – in a cove which is usually referred to as Puffin Bay.

From the landing place in the south-east a path runs along the south coast beaches, climbs slowly to the top of the high cliffs on the west coast, and then turns south-eastwards across the centre of the island, sloping gradually back down towards the Sound of Handa – the ocean channel separating Handa from the mainland. The path is partly paved with duckboarding to try to protect the fragile ground from the effect of 5000 pairs of tramping visitors' feet each year. The remains of the old cottages are alongside the pathway before it reaches the burial ground – some rough weathered headstones in the grass. The Trust's hut is between Bothy Loch, one of Handa's six lochs, all of which have ample water but no fish, and the ruined chapel beside the beach. This clockwise walk of about three-and-a-half miles combines a wonderful view of the startling topography with an astonishing variety of birdlife. Handa supports not only the largest colony of guillemots in Britain but an enormous number of other sea birds, as well as fascinating species such as the great northern diver and the ringed plover. There is a modest charge for visiting the island to help support the work of the Trust. A fitting climax is to circumnavigate the island by boat and see the drama on the cliffs from sea-level.

Opposte: The Great Stack

Toa Rona

RONA

. . .When Mr Morison, the minister, was in Rona, two of the natives courted a maid with intention to marry her; and being married to one of them afterwards, the other was not a little disappointed, because there was no other match for him in this island. The wind blowing fair, Mr Morison sailed directly to Lewis; but after three hours' sailing was forced back to Rona by a contrary wind: and at his landing, the poor man that had lost his sweetheart was overjoyed, and expressed himself in these words: 'I bless God and Ronan that you are returned again, for I hope you will now make me happy, and give me a right to enjoy the woman every other year by turns, that so we both may have issue by her.' Mr Morison could not refrain from smiling at this unexpected request. . .

. . .Another who wanted a wife, and having got a shilling from a seaman that happened to land there, went and gave this shilling to Mr Morison, to purchase him a wife in the Lewis, and send her to him, for he was told that this piece of money was a thing of extraordinary value. . .

Rona is a speck of an island – just 270 acres – lying well north of Lewis in the storm-swept North Atlantic and should not be confused with the Rona which lies alongside Skye. Its situation is every bit as remote and wild as that of St Kilda or Foula although it lacks the dramatic geography of these islands. In 1549 Dean Munro said it was, 'inhabit and manurit be simple people, scant of ony religione' – a people which had continuously inhabited it for 700 years or more.

The first inhabitant was supposed to have been St Ronan in the 8th century but no one is very sure who St Ronan was. There were twelve saints of that name in Donegal and two recorded in Scotland but whether the island was named after – or gave its name to – a saint is anybody's guess. Legend has it that St Ronan's sister, Brianuil, lived with him on Rona until one day Ronan admired her beautiful legs. 'It's time to leave,' she said and went to Sula Sgeir. In Norse 'Rona' means either 'rough island' or 'seal island' and both derivations are equally apt.

The history of the Rona islanders is a graphic example of the fragility of island life. About the mid-1600s the Rev Donald Morison, a minister on Lewis, visited Rona and found five families living in stone and thatched houses, each with a barn, storehouse and cattle-shed. He said they were contented people who took their surname 'from the colour of the sky, rainbow and clouds'. They had no interest in money, using barter if necessary, as they had enough food and clothing for all their needs. They restricted their population to 'thirty souls', by sending their 'supernumerary' people to Lewis.

But a few years after his visit some hungry seamen landed and killed the island's only bull and the ship's rats swam ashore and ate all the food. Within a year 'all that ancient race of people' were dead. The disaster was only discovered when a party from St Kilda (100 miles away!) was shipwrecked on Rona after being blown there by a storm. They lived for seven months on the island while they built a boat out of driftwood which they then sailed to Stornoway.

The island was eventually resettled but by 1796 there was only a shepherd's family left as the rest had drowned in a fishing accident. When MacCulloch landed in 1815 he said the family ran away and hid, because the shepherd, Kenneth MacCagie, with his wife, three children, and old deaf mother, had 'seen no face' for seven years. They thought MacCulloch's party must be 'pirates or Americans', but he managed to persuade them that he meant no harm. They had plenty of food with six or seven acres planted with potatoes and cereals and they lived in a house which was mostly underground. The MacCagies left Rona about 1820 and nine years later John MacDonald went there as a shepherd accompanied by his wife Cirstina and daughter Catherine. They stayed for five years and three more children were born on the island.

The island was more-or-less deserted until 1884 when two men from Ness had a violent argument with their minister and vowed they would never return to the parish. In February 1885 a relief boat called and found them both dead.

Rona was declared a National Nature Reserve in 1956 mainly to protect the 7500 grey seals which breed there every autumn. Nowadays the land supports only sheep which are sheared and tended by a party of Lewis shepherds on an annual visit.

The small, ruined, St Ronan's chapel – partly 'repaired' by Fraser Darling during his sojourn on the island – is listed as one of the three oldest known structures of the Celtic Church and, therefore, possibly the oldest Christian building in Britain. In the burial ground beside it there once stood an ancient stone cross with three holes through it and the much-eroded figure of a naked man carved on it, possibly as a fertility symbol. This cross was removed in the 1930s and placed in Teampull Mholuaidh at Europie on Lewis.

FOULA

. . .There are some rocks here computed to be about three hundred fathoms high, and the way of climbing them is to tie a rope about a man's middle, and let him down with a basket, in which he brings up his eggs and fowl. The Isle of Foula is the most dangerous and fatal to the climbers, for many of them perish in the attempt. . .

Far out in the North Atlantic, almost as near to the Færoe Islands as to Cape Wrath, a small community thrives on the island of Foula – which arguably shares with Fair Isle the distinction of being Scotland's most isolated inhabited outpost.

Like Hirta in the St Kilda group, Foula has towering precipices, an inadequate harbour, its own breed of sheep, and thousands upon thousands of sea birds – which is why the Norsemen named it 'the island of fowls'. But unlike Hirta its islanders are still there, doggedly determined to overcome the difficulties of living in their wild and beautiful home.

When the last 'Queen of Foula', Katherine Asmunder, died in the late 17th century the islanders were still unaware of the introduction of Scots law to Shetland. It was about this time that a ship's surgeon named Scott is said to have visited Foula and persuaded the islanders to hand over their Norse title-deeds on the pretext that he would have them registered in Edinburgh. He had them registered – but in his name – and the Scotts of Melby thus became the legal owners of the island. Similar thefts of land by 'carpetbaggers' from the south were widespread throughout the Northern Isles at that time. Under the Norse udal system crofters were freemen land-owners while under Scots feudal law they became tenants and virtual bondsmen subject to the whims of their landlords. It was not until 1882 that they gained some protection under the Crofting Acts. The one saving grace in Foula's case was that as the islanders were excellent fishermen, and could pay a good rent, they were not 'cleared' for sheep farming.

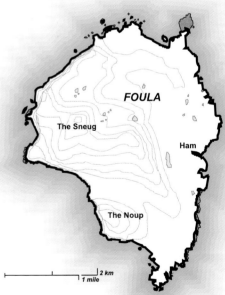

Foula's islanders – there are about forty of them today although a century ago the population numbered nearly 300 – are an independent lot with their own distinctive traditions. For instance, they still use the Julian calendar which the rest of Britain discarded in 1753, and celebrate Christmas and New Year on the 6th and 13th of January respectively. Until 1800 they spoke Norn, a form of the Old Norse language, although it was no longer to be heard anywhere else in Britain and even in 1894 a Færoese linguist was surprised at the close similarity of the island speech to Færoese.

Foula's 'hardback' sheep which were possibly introduced by the Vikings have, in common with all primitive sheep, exceptionally hairy fleeces and the island has another point of distinction, its own sub-species of field mouse, a charming little creature with big feet. The land rises from east to west with a low, broken coastline in the east and precipitous sandstone cliffs rising to a height of 365 metres in the west. These cliffs are unequalled throughout the British Isles in their sheer dramatic impact even if they just fail (by two metres) to match the height of the awesome St Kildan cliffs: but with five distinct peaks, many rock stacks, and vertiginous cliffs, Foula can provide a wealth of excitement for mountaineers.

At one time the menfolk of Foula were almost entirely engaged in fishing but nowadays crofting has had to take precedence. All the crofts are on the east side which has, actually, some of the best arable land in Shetland. About half the population live at Ham near Ham Voe, 'harbour inlet' in Old Norse, where there is a post-office, a school (rebuilt at considerable expense), a church and a 'smiddy' selling local crafts.

In easterlies great waves come crashing into Ham Voe so the fishing boats have to be beached high above sea-level at the head of the narrow little voe. A monthly mailboat service began in 1879 after the local minister had written to Queen Victoria and received a reply from Disraeli, but 'monthly' was an optimistic term as passengers and goods had to be landed on the rocks which was only possible in reasonable weather. It was not until the country was at war in 1914 that a tiny concrete pier was built which included a step for a gun emplacement. Many years later a power-driven crane and winch were added to allow the mailboat to be lifted out instead of being manhandled onto the pier. The present service from Walls on Mainland Shetland is still entirely dependent on the weather and there have been many problems in recent years because officials purchased a new ferry which was not designed to cope with the severe conditions. Even today there are occasions when bad weather can cut off island access for up to six weeks at a time.

The Noup of Foula

Vaila Hall

VAILA

. . . The inhabitants of the isle Vaila say that no cat will live in it, and if any cat be brought to it, they will rather venture to sea, than stay in the isle. They say that a cat was seen upon the isle about fifty years ago; but how it came there was unknown. They observed about the same time, how the proprietor was in great torment, and as they supposed by witchcraft, of which they say he then died. There is no account that any cat has been seen in the isle ever since that gentleman's death except when they were carried to it, for making the above-mentioned experiment. . .

Islands are a fertile ground for human eccentricity. The wild extravagances of late-Victorian industrialists such as Sir George Bullough on Rum are probably better known than those of Herbert Anderton on Vaila but there are many similarities.

When Anderton, a rich Yorkshire mill-owner on a wool-buying business trip to Shetland in 1893, saw Vaila, he liked it, bought it, and immediately set about creating a mini-kingdom. There was a semi-derelict but fine stone house on the 800-acre island which had been built in 1696 by a local merchant, James Mitchell of Scalloway. Anderton set about turning this building into the largest 'country-house' in Shetland. The original house became the south wing of Vaila Hall and the original entrance doorway with the Mitchell coat-of-arms and date above it was retained. The north wing of the Hall was reconstructed from the various outbuildings while a central courtyard became the hall itself. Some of the stone and skilled labour for the work was imported from England and many of the ornaments and contents came from further afield as Anderton's work had often taken him abroad. The stone griffons flanking the entrance steps, for instance, are thought to have come from Germany.

There were also other reconstruction projects. Both Anderton and his wife were keen artists and his brother was a Royal Academician so a studio was combined with the boathouse at the east pier and as he had a Buddha from Japan among his many artefacts he constructed a small Buddhist temple beside the studio. On the other side of the island, within sight of Vaila Hall, an ancient two-storey watch tower became a folly with added crenellations and an angle turret. New farm buildings were constructed on the fertile ground in the north of the island and the farm was stocked with sheep, Clydesdale horses,

131

dairy cattle and a large herd of quality Shetland ponies, creating work for about a dozen families.

As soon as Vaila Hall was completed it became the Anderton's summer residence with accommodation for many large parties of house guests. As befitted an island laird, a brass cannon made in Yorkshire was ceremoniously fired from the terrace whenever the Andertons arrived on Vaila.

Sadly, by the 1930s, the stock-market slump brought an end to the good times and Anderton's fortune largely disappeared as he struggled to keep his businesses afloat. He retired full-time to the island in 1933 and lived there in virtual isolation until he died in 1937. Years followed in which the whole property deteriorated steadily until, in 1969, it was partly rescued by a grand-nephew, Henry Anderton, and then by the present owners who bought the island from him in 1993.

Herbert Anderton was not the only remarkable character to have a connection with Vaila. There was also Arthur Anderson (a confusing similarity of names!), who was born in Shetland in 1792 – a 'beach-boy' (fish-drier) who acquired some education and volunteered to join the Navy. He became a midshipman and, in due course, a Captain's clerk. He then left the Navy and obtained employment with a London shipowner, Willcox, who eventually offered him a partnership. Together, he and Willcox started the Peninsular Steam Company in 1837 which, three years later, became the famous Peninsular and Oriental Line – 'P & O' – running regular mail services to India and China. It was in that same year, 1837, that he also established the Shetland Fishery Company on the island of Vaila – with the innovation that the fishermen should have shared ownership of their boats and catches. It was in the following year that he started the regular steamship mail-service to Shetland which still exists today in the form of P & O ferries serving the Northern Isles.

Anderson had many interests. He travelled widely, intervened successfully in a civil war in Portugal, founded a Home for Sailors' Widows and a Liberal newspaper in Shetland, and presented Queen Victoria with a fine knitted Shetland shawl which instantly appealed to fashion-conscious London society and created a new cottage industry.

This untiring and benevolent man was a Liberal MP for Orkney and Shetland for several years. He always retained a great sense of humour and although his first love was Shetland his outlook was far from insular – for instance, he suggested the construction of a Suez canal long before De Lessops came on the scene.

Arthur Anderson, who died aged seventy-seven, may have had only a passing connection with the island of Vaila but the island gains much by association with one of the truly great Shetlanders.

PAPA STOUR

. . . Papa-Stour is two miles in length; it excels any isle of its extent for all the conveniences of human life: it has four good harbours, one of which looks to the south, another to the west, and two to the north. . .

Each volcanic island being formed today off the coast of Iceland will become a Papa Stour tomorrow. The soft ash is eaten away by the sea from its hard volcanic base creating tunnels and arches and grotesque, tortuous shapes. On the surface, where the sea cannot wash it away, seeds take root in the lava and the ash is converted into fertile soil, rich in essential nutrients.

Thought to have been first settled about 3000BC, Papa Stour is one of the most fertile of the Shetland Islands. It has a precipitous coastline, indented and eroded, above a tumble of detached rocks, stacks and skerries – a wonderland for divers and potholers. In the north-west, for instance, beneath the highest hill, Virda Field, a natural tunnel called the Hole of Bordie is nearly one kilometre in length and beyond the Stack of Snalda the Fogla and Lyra Skerries have subterranean passages through which the tide surges powerfully.

There are many sea-caves including what is arguably Britain's finest – Kirstan's (or Christie's) Hole – which is at the head of a narrow creek and confined between vertical rock faces about thirty metres high. A huge natural arch forms the entrance leading to an enclosed space with glistening walls standing open to the sky. The cave continues for about another seventy metres, ending at a beach. Another cave, Francie's Hole, is smaller than Kirstan's Hole but possibly more beautiful. The perfectly arched entrance leads to a 'fairyland, so exquisite is the colouring of the roof and sides' with dark side caverns and a small pink beach at the back with alcoves above it.

When the Norsemen came they presumably found monks in residence because it was they who named it Papa Stour – the 'big island of the priests'. Archaeologists recently found what is almost certainly the 13th-century residence of Duke Haakon, later King of Norway, who had a farm on the island beside Housa Voe. Hanseatic merchants later considered the 200-acre island of sufficient importance to warrant a summer trading booth and in the 19th century a herring station was constructed to which curers and gutters came from far afield,

even from Ireland. Fuel was so scarce and the fishermen so busy that the islanders started burning the rich turf for fuel. Large areas still lie scalped and bare today and with the decline in herring stocks the situation became so bad that people started to leave.

By 1970 the school had closed and the total population, which had been nearly 400 in the 1840s was only sixteen fairly elderly people. Tides rage through the narrow Sound of Papa which can isolate the island for days at a time but after a newspaper advertisement offered free crofts with five sheep each there was an immediate response. Papa Stour was suddenly seen as a refuge from the rat-race and Shetlanders started calling it the 'Hippy Isle'. Most of the newcomers gave up quickly when they discovered the rigours rather than the romance of island existence but a few remained and brought new life although the island still teeters on the brink of depopulation.

The stacks and inlets support many sea birds but it is interesting to learn that although the fulmar is relatively widespread now, in 1890 an ornithologist visiting Papa Stour noted with delight that he had actually seen one.

All the habitation is in the east, mainly around Housa Voe where there is a pier for the small ferryboat from West Burra Firth on Mainland. Outside the voe there is an isolated rock stack with the vestige of a stone house perched on its narrow top – the Maiden or Frau Stack. This is said to have been built in the early 14th century by Lord Thorvald Thoresson for his daughter to live in to ensure her virginity – but all to no avail for she still became pregnant.

Papa Stour's mood changes with the weather and when a haar creeps in and blankets the wicks and geos it can have an almost sinister quality. But with the sun comes magic and it is said that fishermen can locate the island in a summer haar by the pungent smell of its wild flowers – 'Fir da scent o flooers in Papa leds wis aa da wye'.

Kirstan's Hole, Papa Stour

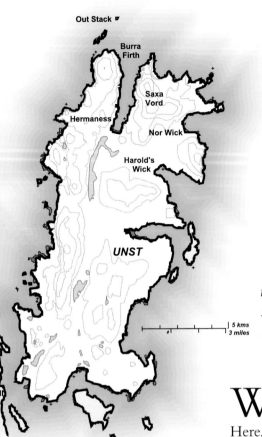

Out Stack

Burra
Firth

Saxa
Vord

Hermaness

Nor Wick

Harold's
Wick

UNST

5 kms
3 miles

U N S T

...The isle of Unst is eight miles long, and is the pleasantest of the Shetland isles; it has three churches and as many harbours; it is reckoned the most northern of all the British Dominions...

...The inhabitants...generally speak the English tongue, and many among them retain the ancient Danish language, especially in the more northern isles. There are several who speak English, Norse, and Dutch; the last of which is acquired by their converse with the Hollanders, that fish yearly in those isles...

We often hear the length of Britain described as 'Land's End to John O' Groats' but the end of the road is nearly 200 miles further north – on the lovely island of Unst. Here, in the extreme north, at Wick of Skaw, is Britain's most northerly dwelling – a croft farmhouse overlooking great banks of marsh marigolds in a small green valley by the sea. One of the outhouses is made from an old upturned boat – normal island practice where nothing is wasted.

Not far away there is a road leading to the summit of Saxa Vord, Unst's highest point at 284 metres. From this breathtaking viewpoint the most northerly land of the British Isles – Out Stack (or 'Oosta') – is less than two miles away. Beyond it the stormy sea stretches uninterrupted all the way to the Arctic. In 1849 Lady Franklin landed on this dangerous rock to pray for her husband when he failed to return from his Northwest Passage expedition. Slightly nearer, and set on a clump of skerries surrounded by wheeling sea-birds, is the famous lighthouse of Muckle Flugga, built by David Stevenson in 1858 and now automated. Robert Louis Stevenson visited Unst when his Uncle David had finished the construction. Soon after this he started writing *Treasure Island* and it is interesting to note how his map of Treasure Island resembles the map of Unst

As I said, Unst is a lovely island. I admit to having seen it in bright sunshine, which colours

Skaw, the last house in Britain

the memory, but our Northern Isles are not given sufficient credit for their dry, sunny days. Days without wind are another matter. In 1962 an all-British wind speed record of 177mph was recorded on Saxa Vord although it was never given official recognition because the anemometer blew away.

The north coast of Unst's spectacular coastline is interrupted by the deep cleft - beautiful but ominous – of Burra Firth. The peninsula on the west side, Hermaness National Nature Reserve, is a wild rugged area maintained by Scottish Natural Heritage. The cliffs here are home to one of our largest sea-bird colonies, many thousands of fulmar, gannet, kittiwake, guillemot, razorbill and puffin, with a small number of Arctic skua and almost too many bonxie, or great skua – if one can say that about a bird which was at one time nearing extinction.

It was to these cliffs that a famous black-browed albatross, first seen in the early 1970s, used to return each spring. A vagrant from the South Seas and trapped in the northern hemisphere the poor lonely thing kept hoping, for some twenty long years, to find a mate. It would occasionally wink hopefully at a passing gannet but this always ended in a violent rebuff.

Being in the far north Unst is, naturally, a land of giants. Many years ago a giant called Saxi lived in his Haa by the Vord. Herman was another giant who inhabited the other side of the Burra Firth but they were unfriendly neighbours and always quarrelling. One day, Herman, using a ship's mast as a fishing rod, caught a whale for supper and as it was such a large catch he asked Sax to boil it for him in his kettle. Saxi's Kettle is a huge rock-cup in Nor Wick through which the tide boils and gurgles. Saxi agreed provided he could keep half of it for himself but Herman thought this was unfair. The quarrel became heated and before long the giants were throwing stones at each other. One of the huge stones which Herman threw is still lying on the west side of Saxa Vord and a stone which Saxi threw fell into the sea and became a skerry (Saxi's Baa) on the west shore of Burra Firth.

Scandinavian pirates or 'vikings' probably first settled in the Northern Isles about AD600/700 and became so well established that they started raiding their old Norse homeland. King Harald Haarfagr ('fair-haired Harald') sailed over with a small fleet in 875 to put a stop to the piracy and annex the islands as Norwegian possessions. He anchored for a time in this bay on Unst which was named after him.

In the south Unst has a handsome but desolate ruined castle at Muness which was built in 'the zeir of God 1598', according to the inscription, by the evil Lawrence Bruce, a relative of Earl Patrick. It is worth seeing. There is a flavour of Transylvania about it, or possibly Edgar Allan Poe, and it was burned down within a century of being built.

In keeping with this litany of extremes, Haroldswick, on Unst, has the most northerly post-office in Britain which is always happy to frank your letters accordingly. This may be the end of the northern road – but there couldn't be a more fitting climax to any journey.

FETLAR

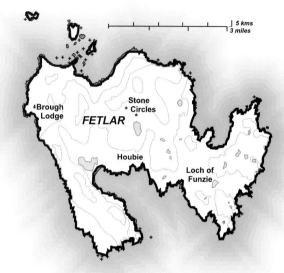

. . . The isle of Fetlor lies to the north-east of Yell; . . . it has a church, and some of the Picts houses in it. . .

. . . The inhabitants say that if a compass be placed at the house of Udsta, on the west side of the isle Fetlor, the needle will be in perpetual disorder, without fixing to any one pole; and that being tried afterwards on the top of that house, it had the same effect. They add further that when a vessel sails near that house, the needle of the compass is disordered in the same manner. . .

Fetlar is probably most renowned by bird-watchers for the snowy owls found nesting at Stackaberg in 1967. Unfortunately the cantankerous old male, having driven off all the young suitors, died of old age in 1975 and left several morose females without a mate. As a result there are now no more snowy owls nesting in Shetland although they do occasionally come visiting from Scandinavia.

Fetlar is an outstanding bird sanctuary so my wife, Jean, and I were lucky to have had the late Bobby Tulloch as our guide. As a Shetlander, RSPB warden, noted ornithologist, wildlife photographer and, above all, a wonderful character with a wealth of tales, we couldn't have been in better hands. We were accompanied by six fanatical bird-watchers which suited us perfectly as, whenever they settled down for a prolonged study, it gave us an opportunity to sketch. Apart from that, however, we were keen to see a red-necked phalarope – because, if nothing else, it has such a wonderful name – and Bobby didn't let us down. We stood beside the Loch of Funzie and this strange and fearless little bird waded right past us; no more than six feet away.

The story of Fetlar goes back a long way. The first Norse settlers are thought to have made landfall here, and swashbuckling King Harald the Fair-haired visited the island during his pursuit of 'vikings' in the 9th century. This is Shetland's most fertile island and more than 200 different species of wild flower have been recorded including rarities such as the frog orchid, the northern gentian and some unique sedges.

The Norsemen never arrived at a suitable definition for an island and they spoke of Fetlar as Est Isle and Wast Isle, probably because a mini-Great Wall of China divided the

Brough Lodge, Fetlar

island in half and no one was sure who had built it. Its creation was attributed to the Finns, magical figures in Norse folklore, who might have been Laplanders, or giants, or trolls, or all three rolled together. It was said that the Finns built the wall in a single night in exchange for a farmer's best cow.

Today, the mysterious one-metre wide wall, or what little is left of it, is still called Funzie Girt (pron. *fin-ee gurt*) which means the Finns' dyke. There are other mysteries too such as the Fiddler's Crus. These are three stone circles set in a cabalistic triangular pattern and almost touching each other. Each circle is about thirteen-and-a-half metres in diameter. Nearby there is another strange monument called Hjaltadans (which means 'limping dance'). This is an outer circle of thirty-eight serpentine stones, about eleven-and-a-half metres diameter, with an internal, low and concentric earth bank. Two stones lie at the centre. Both these structures seem to be related but archaeologists have no satisfactory explanation of their purpose. The local belief is that a fiddler and his wife were dancing in the moonlight one night with trolls and were enjoying it so much that they failed to notice the dawn. They were all petrified by the light of the rising sun and the stone circles are the dancing trolls and the two prostrate central stones are the fiddler and his wife.

Fetlar is surrounded with shipwrecks. In 1737 under the magnificent eastern cliffs of serpentine stone a Danish ship, *Wendela*, carrying a large quantity of unspecified silver currency, ran aground and sank. Most of the coins were immediately salvaged by the islanders but in the 1970s an official diving team investigated the wreck and collected a number of silver coins which had been overlooked (unauthorised diving is forbidden, by the way).

A Fetlar man, Sir William Watson Cheyne of Leagarth House at Houbie, went on to become a famous surgeon after assisting Joseph Lister in the development of antiseptic surgery. The Fetlar Centre which is almost opposite Leagarth House is a treasure trove of island history and Houbie itself is a delightful spot – but don't use a compass in the bay as the sand is magnetic.

The first large-scale clearances in Shetland started on Fetlar in 1822 when the owner, Sir Arthur Nicolson, evicted the crofters to make room for sheep. By 1858 he had emptied the whole of the north and west part of the island and cleared more than half the population. Using stone from the evicted crofters' houses he then built himself a three-storey tower folly, Brough Lodge.

The broch of Mousa

MOUSA

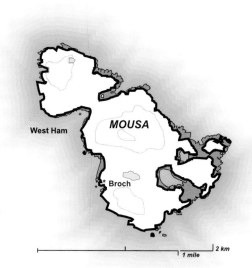

...There are many Picts' houses in this country, and several of them entire to this day; the highest exceeds not twenty or thirty feet in height, and are about twelve feet broad in the middle; they taper towards both ends, the entry is lower than the doors of houses commonly are now, the windows are long and very narrow, and the stairs go up between the walls. These houses were built for watch-towers, to give notice of an approaching enemy; there is not one of them but is in view of some other; so that a fire being made on the top of any one house the signal was communicated to all the rest in a few moments...

Mousa – the 'mossy island' with a world-renowned broch – is, believe it or not, our most romantic island. Or at least it certainly was at one time.

The famous broch is about 2000 years old and, although it has lost some of its upper courses, it is still a remarkable example of the craft of the ancient builders. Fifteen metres in diameter at ground level, the double walls curve gracefully inwards to an upper diameter of about twelve metres. It is built of small slate-like stones meticulously laid dry to give a smooth exterior with stairs between the walls which lead up through six galleries to a height of thirteen-and-a-half metres. The workmanship is quite remarkable when one remembers that timber was exceptionally scarce and that the curved walls were probably built without templates and depending on the good eye of the stonemason. In fact the quality is such that it seems as though the builders have just packed up their tools and gone home for the night.

At the time of the Vikings – say, 900 years ago – the circular internal courtyard of the broch contained a 'wheelhouse' which had probably been added in the 2nd or 3rd century. It's still there today. A 'wheelhouse' is an Iron Age dwelling with rooms set out like the spokes of a wheel.

Mousa's first romantic episode took place about AD900. Over in Norway a young man, Bjorn, fell in love with a girl called Thora Jewel-hand. Her parents disapproved so the couple eloped and he took her to his parent's house on the Sogne Fjord where she stayed throughout the winter – virtue intact. In the spring Bjorn's father gave him a trading-ship and suggested that he should make for Dublin where business was good. His parents wanted Thora to remain with them until his return but she would have none of it and insisted on going with him. A violent storm blew up and they were nearly drowned but they managed at last to run the broken ship aground on Mousa. While the crew set about repairing it the young lovers married and turned the ancient broch into their honeymoon home.

The following spring news came that Thora's parents had persuaded King Harald of Norway to outlaw Bjorn. As his ship was now ready for sea Bjorn and Thora decided they must set sail immediately for Iceland. When they arrived they were made welcome and a few months later Thora produced a daughter called Asgerd – and they all lived happily ever after.

A couple of centuries later Mousa again appeared in the Norse sagas. This time the tale is of Margaret, the daughter of Earl Haakon, who had been married to the elderly Earl Maddad of Atholl for more than twenty years and had an adult son – Earl Harald. When Earl Maddad died the mature but beautiful Margaret shocked the neighbours by immediately moving in with young Gunni Asleifsson. Mercurial and oversexed Margaret soon became pregnant but didn't want to raise another family so, as soon as she had given birth to the child (in 1153) she set Gunni up as a lone parent and turned her attention instead on a handsome young man from Shetland, Earl Erland Ungi, son of Harald the Fair-spoken. Erland was enthralled and swept her off to his private shack – the broch on Mousa. Here the couple established their love nest and, although the broch does not look particularly cosy by present-day standards, no doubt love overcame all discomforts. At least the chosen spot was private and defensible, which was important as it was not long before Margaret's twenty-year-old son, Earl Harald Maddadson, besieged it. He was most upset and enraged by his mother's unladylike behaviour but after many petulant months spent in miserable weather outside the broch he still could not breach its defences. In the end his anger wore off and he agreed to forgive them both provided Erland made his mother an honest woman by marrying her. The couple agreed and were married and the saga ends in the best Hollywood tradition because after the ceremony Harald invited them aboard his boat and sailed them over to Norway for a legitimate honeymoon.

FAIR ISLE

. . . There are fine hawks in these isles, and particularly those of Fair Isle are reputed among the best that are to be had anywhere; they are observed to go far for their prey, and particularly for moorfowl as far as the isles of Orkney, which are about sixteen leagues from them. . .

. . . There are likewise many eagles in and about these isles, which are very destructive to the sheep and lambs. . .

. . . The crows are very numerous. and differ in colour from those on the mainland; for the head, wings, and tail. . . are only black, and their back, breast, and tail of a grey colour. When black crows are seen there at any time the inhabitants say it is a presage of approaching famine. . .

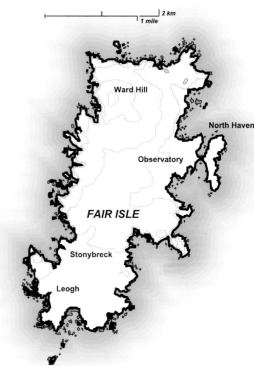

Seen from the sea, when the weather is clear, Fair Isle has a distinctive outline – a low, bare southern coastline sloping up to high northern cliffs studded with natural arches, stacks and other interesting red-sandstone formations. But it is not always so easy to see and a survey has shown that, since records began and up to the advent of radar, there was, on average, a major shipwreck on these rocks every four to five years! Its lonely location – almost half-way between the two great northern archipelagoes of Shetland and Orkney – didn't help, and this may have accounted for its name which is thought to be a corruption of 'Far Isle'.

One of these shipwrecks was well-documented. In 1588 an auxiliary flagship in the Spanish Armada, the thirty-eight-gun *El Gran Grifon*, withstood an attack by Sir Francis Drake's *Revenge*, and escaped into unknown northern waters. Several short summer nights later there was a sudden squall and she ran blindly onto the rocks of Fair Isle at Sivars Geo on the south-east side. About 200 men survived the catastrophe and struggled ashore but they had been wthout food for several days and were weak from hunger. The islanders fed them but the Spaniards were dissatisfied and started raiding the winter stocks, killing poultry and slaughtering the precious cattle and sheep. In desperation, the islanders persuaded the sailors to board a ship bound for Shetland where, as Scotland was not at war with Spain, the men were well-fed and well-treated until they were repatriated. To commemorate this event, a Spanish delegation dressed as conquistadors visited Fair Isle in 1984 and dedicated an iron cross in the island's kirkyard to those who had died.

Fair Isle is, of course, world-renowned for its distinctive, non-repetitive knitwear patterns and these are sometimes said to have been introduced by the shipwrecked Spanish sailors of *El Gran Grifon*. I would think this is most unlikely and that the patterns are clearly a development of traditional Nordic designs. Norsemen were settled here, after all, long before any Spaniards appeared.

Like so many of our islands, the population of Fair Isle was steadily dwindling between the two World Wars and the time was approaching when it would be yet another beautiful but uninhabited island. It was saved from this fate by a keen ornithologist called George Waterston who visited it in 1935 and was so enthralled by its birdlife that he made several more visits before being called up for active service in 1939. He was later captured by the Germans and it was while he was a prisoner of war that he first seriously dreamed of purchasing the island and starting a bird observatory. As soon as the war was over he set about gaining international recognition for Fair Isle by publicising its extremely varied birdlife – over 345 species, more than anywhere else in Britain – and by 1948 he had achieved his ambition of buying the island and founding the Fair Isle Bird Observatory. The immediate effect was to stop the population drain by giving the small but thriving island community another good reason to remain in their beautiful 2000-acre realm.

Apart from those directly involved with the Nature Reserve, in community service, or knitting, the main occupation is, and always was, crofting, supplemented by some fishing. Dykes cross the island – the Hill Dyke and the ancient Feelie Dyke – to keep the sheep which graze the northern hills out of the cultivated southern fields. The majority of the seventy islanders live in the south where the scattered settlement of Stonybreck includes a post-office, general store, school, museum and two churches. But the Observatory, the airstrip and the main harbour – North Haven, which is the port for the passenger ferry, *The Good Shepherd* – are in the north.

In 1954 the National Trust for Scotland took over Waterston's good work and built the mail-boat pier at North Haven, good communications being the essential ingredient for any viable island community. North Haven is a secure, but very restricted little harbour. The Trust also improved much of the property including the Bird Observatory and Hostel which was rebuilt in 1969 with accommodation for twenty-four visitors.

Ornithologists to date have ringed about a quarter of a million birds of some eighty different species including even an occasional Lapland bunting, barred warbler and pied woodpecker. Visitors are always welcome although ornithologists naturally have prior choice of accommodation. For bird watchers, in particular, this is the opportunity of a lifetime but beware of the bonxies during the breeding season as they are expert and savage dive-bombers!

. . . beware of the bonxies. . .

Hasuell-Smith

SANDAY

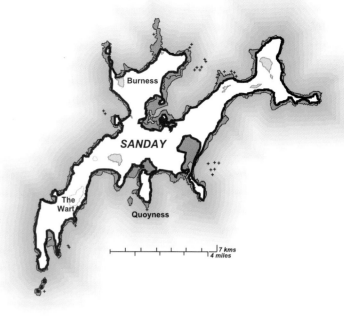

. . . The isle Sanda lies north, twelve miles in length, and is reckoned the most fruitful and beautiful of all the Orcades. . .

. . . The sheep are very fruitful here, many of them have two, some three, and others four lambs at a time; they often die with a disease called the sheep-dead, which is occasioned by little animals about half an inch long, that are engendered in their liver. . .

. . . In the chapel of Clet, in the isle of Sanda, there is a grave of nineteen feet in length; some who had the curiosity to open it, found only a piece of a man's backbone in it, bigger than that of a horse. The minister of the place had the curiosity to keep the bone by him for some time. The inhabitants have a tradition of a giant there whose stature was such that he could reach his hand as high as the top of the chapel. . .

At sea-level in dark misty weather this low-lying, sprawling Orkney island of 12,500 acres is virtually invisible and, consequently, before the days of radar, there was a constant supply of shipwrecks to keep the inhabitants warm. There is no peat so wooden ships were very welcome and it is even said that there were prayers in church asking the Lord for assistance in this respect.

The island's long coastline divides into a large number of shallow and exposed bays with beautiful wide white sandy beaches. These are usually deserted except for multitudes of wading birds including bar-tailed godwit, dunlin and turnstone. Birdlife here is prolific with corncrake and corn bunting, colonies of Arctic tern and many ringed plover.

Sanday is the island of sand – Norse and English have the same word – and from a comparison with old maps it appears that the sandbanks are slowly being extended by the sea. In other words, unlike some other parts of the British Isles, this is a growing island.

The light, sandy soil is very fertile and the bedrock is a well-weathered sandstone of a pleasant pinkish-grey colour. The sand is tied down at the coasts by the roots of marram grass although thousands of rabbits do their best to disturb the delicate balance. Kelp was the major industry in the 18th century as the island produced one quarter of Orkney's total

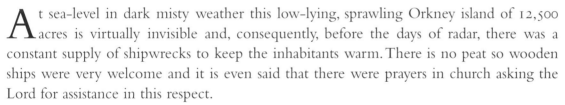

Inside the chambered cairn at Quoyness

149

production and even when the kelp boom died it was of little concern as farming took over and the farms were the most prosperous in Orkney. The main problem for the farmers is water because, although there are a few small lochs, sandy soil is not good at retaining moisture. The productive farming is supplemented by lobster fishing and seaweed-gathering for alginate processing. This is a thriving community of over 500 friendly people and for the visitor the island is also a beachcomber's delight. For additional diversion, there is even a challenging golf course among the dunes of the Plain of Fidge.

Few visible ancient monuments interrupt the agricultural landscape although almost every ness has the faint trace of a broch. The exception is Els Ness, which at one time would have been a separate island but is now connected by an 'ayre' or isthmus. It is spattered with cairns like inverted craters on the surface of the moon. One of these is the beautifully constructed chambered cairn at Quoyness which has a spacious central chamber and six cells. It is the largest of such cairns to have been excavated in Orkney and bones found in it have been radiocarbon dated to about 2300BC.

Stone Age burial mounds were treated with respect by the old crofters. This is because every mound has a resident hogboon and, as everyone knows, hogboons are very bad-tempered, untrustworthy and troublesome. At Hellihowe on Sanday, for example, one hogboon was such a pest that the desperate farmer was forced in the end to sell his croft and move elsewhere, but as he carried his possessions into his new crofthouse the hogboon stuck its head out of a kirn and said: 'We're gettan a fine day tae flit on, guidman.'

Maybe the most interesting relic yet found is that of a Viking ship-burial at the north end of the Burness peninsula. This was discovered in 1991 when one side of the boat, which is six-and-a-half metres long, had already been washed away by the sea. But the remaining half contained a compartment with the skeletal remains of a man, a woman and a child. Beside the man was a sword, a quiver of arrows and some bone gaming pieces while the woman had two spindle whorls, a pair of shears, and some iron objects which may be parts from a wooden box. There was also a decorated whalebone plaque, a sickle, and a brooch.

The twenty-ton Saville Stone is near here. Legend claims that this great rock was thrown by a furious witch on Eday at a man on Sanday with whom her daughter had eloped. She missed him and the couple lived happily ever after. The stone's true origin is actually from much further away than the island of Eday as it is a block of Scandinavian gneiss which has been carried across the North Sea by a glacier during the Ice Age.

EDAY

. . . To the north of the main lies the isle of. . . Eda which is four miles in length. . .

. . . The fields everywhere abound with variety of plants and roots, and the latter are generally very large; the common people dress their leather with the roots of tormentil, instead of bark. . . Their common fuel is peat and turf, of which there is such plenty as to furnish a salt-pan with fuel. A south-east and north-west moon cause high water here. . .

In early November, 1724, a trading ship, the *George*, put in to the pirate-ridden Barbery coast of North Africa to collect a load of beeswax bound for Genoa. The second mate on board was a young Orcadian called John Gow who was ambitious but by no means bright. He had seen and admired the lifestyle of the local pirates and decided that the sooner he became a pirate, and roamed the seven seas in his own ship, the better. So he organised a mutiny in which the captain and three of the crew were murdered, took command of the *George*, renamed it *Revenge*, and set off in search of adventure.

Once clear of the Mediterranean he captured several innocent merchantmen but in each case found to his disgust that their cargo was only Newfoundland dried cod so he decided to sail north and try his luck in home waters. On reaching Orkney, he first anchored off Stromness and raided Clestrain House but the raid was a failure so, for consolation, he crossed over to the little island of Cava and kidnapped some girls for a few days. After this diversion he sailed north to Eday where he remembered that one of his old schoolfellows, James Fea, came from a wealthy family and lived in considerable comfort in Carrick House overlooking Calf Sound.

But Gow, as usual, made a mess of it. He had forgotten how treacherous the Orkney tides could be and his ship ran aground almost in front of Carrick House. James Fea saw the mishap, possibly with some amusement, but then saw an armed party coming ashore. He had plenty of time to organise a suitable reception, capture the raiding party and take Gow prisoner. That was in February 1725 so Gow's illustrious career as a pirate had lasted only four months! Fea handed Gow over to the authorities and appropriated his ship's bell which is still kept in Carrick House. In due course the inept pirate was hanged at Execution Dock but even his death was a farce as the rope broke. However, the hangman

Carrick House, Eday

merely gave him a friendly pat on the back and hanged him again, this time successfully.

Carrick House was built about a century before this event. The youthful John Stewart, second son of the unpopular Earl Robert Stewart of Orkney, was accused of associating with a witch called Alysoun Balfour and poisoning his brother Patrick. Alysoun was tortured but John was acquitted, created Earl of Carrick, and granted the island of Eday. He immediately set about building a home and the date 1633 can still be seen inscribed over the courtyard gateway. The house has a delightful setting, its own home farm and some pleasant woodland filled with the song of migrant birds in spring and autumn. A number of prehistoric chambered cairns run south from Carrick House to the unusual and distinctive standing Stone of Setter, which is almost an Eday icon. The great stone stands near Mill Loch, where rare red-throated divers can be seen among the reeds.

Eday is a long island of about 6800 acres with a narrow waist. This is aptly described by its Norse name which means 'isthmus island'. It can be dark and bleak when the skies are grey for the ridge of hills running down the spine is clothed in a deep layer of peat moor-land. This is particularly good peat and Eday used to supply the islands of Sanday and North Ronaldsay with most of their fuel require-ments. Eday peat was also exported to a number of whisky distilleries throughout Scotland. Nowadays the moors, dotted with bog myrtle – a plant which is found nowhere else in Orkney, are mainly used for rough grazing by sheep and regularly burned to encourage the growth of young heather.

The extent of the moorland means that only the narrow coastal strip and the southern part of the island are cultivated, mainly with small owner-occupied farms. A road runs southwards for the entire length of the island, from Calf Sound, past London Airport – the modern airstrip – and many prehistoric chambered cairns, to the standing stone at Southside. Travelling down this road gives a true flavour of Eday's wide skies and ancient windswept landscape.

Although the ferry route leads through Calf Sound in the north the ferry pier is at Backaland in the south-east. At least the ferries are well aware of the strength of the tides in Calf Sound!

Old Man
of Hoy

* Dwarfie
Stane

HOY

Lyness

Longhope

Melsetter
House

5 kms
3 miles

HOY

. . . Over against Kerston Bay lie the isles of Hoy and Waes, which make
but one isle, about twelve miles in length, and mountainous. In this island
is the hill of Hoy, which is reckoned the highest in Orkney. . .
. . . The inhabitants say there are mines of silver, tin, and lead. . .
. . . The sea abounds with variety of fish, but especially herrmg, which
are much neglected since the battle of Kilsyth, at which time the fishermen
from Fife were almost all killed there. . .

One of the first sights to greet any ferry-traveller to Orkney is the Old Man of Hoy
and several miles of the most awe-inspiring sea cliffs in Britain. But this is not typical.
The Norsemen named it Hoy - meaning, quite simply, 'high island' - because this is the only
'high' island in Orkney. The ground rises in three wild, rugged, rain-swept masses divided
by deep gaps, and the bedrock is a beautiful hard sandstone unique to Hoy and known to
geologists as Upper Old Red Sandstone. It weathers slowly into massive, sharp, geometrical
slabs which are an irresistible temptation for any mountaineer. As for the Old Man himself,
appreciate him while you can, because that great 120-metre column of sandstone is balanced precariously on a soft lava layer which is steadily being eaten away by the sea. Sooner
or later – sometime in the next few centuries – the Old Man is going to fall.

Legends abound in Hoy's cloudy mountain passes. This is a land of trolls and goblins,
dwarfs and giants   the 'Misty Mountains' of Tolkien's *Lord of the Rings*. Here a huge block
of red sandstone – 28 feet by 14 feet by 6 feet high – called the Dwarfie Stane lies within
a natural amphitheatre, the Dwarfie Hamars. A passage with two chambers has been carved
inside the stone creating what archaeologists believe is the only example in Northern
Europe of the rock-cut chamber tombs of the Mediterranean. It probably dates from about
2000BC and, of course, it may not be a tomb. Martin Martin thought it had a domestic
purpose – 'at one of the ends. . . there is cut out a bed and pillow capable of two persons
to lie in, at the other end there is a void space cut out resembling a bed, and above both
these there is a large hole which is supposed was a vent for smoke. The common tradition
is that a giant and his wife made this their place of retreat.' Sir Walter Scott, on the other

Opposite: The Old Man of Hoy

154

hand, considered the owner to be a troll or ogre rather than a giant. He claimed that 'the necromantic owner may sometimes still be seen sitting by the Dwarfie Stone'. Certainly the mysterious Trowie Glen, home of the trolls, is nearby and the Dwarfie Hamars themselves are named after the dwarfs who, as everyone knows, are excellent miners and metal-workers and forged Thor's famous hammer.

The track of roadway which passes the Dwarfie Stane runs from the village of Hoy to the Atlantic coast at Rackwick. This picturesque old fishing village, stretching up the glen from a pebble beach, is Orkney's most isolated spot. The school closed in 1954 and the population has faded away but some of the cottages are reinhabited by visitors in the summer months and the famous composer, Peter Maxwell Davies, lives and composes in a converted croft in the hills above the village. Many years ago the men of Rackwick were known as fine fishermen and even finer country dancers. They cheerfully walked four miles over the ghostly hills to Hoy village, danced the night through, and then walked home again in time for the fishing.

Hoy is a treasure-house of plantlife, by far the best in Orkney, including a number of rare alpines, and it is also reputed to support Orkney's only grasshoppers. North Hoy is an RSPB Reserve and a marvellous variety of bird species can be seen – if you can survive the midges.

Most of the north is now sadly depopulated. The main road runs down the east coast to Lyness which was the headquarters for the Scapa Flow naval base during World War II and home to about 30,000 men. The south of Hoy is more green and mellow than the north and has an active farming community. Melsetter House at the head of Longhope is one of Orkney's finest historic buildings and worth a visit. It is an old laird's house which was enlarged in the late 19th century in the style of William Morris with furniture designed by Maddox Brown and Gabriel Rosetti.

Each ness enclosing the secluded harbour of Longhope has a Martello Tower – broch-like structure built for protection against US privateers during the Napoleonic War of 1813-5. A century later, they were armed again for the first World War.

ISLE
OF MAY

. . . It comes in the month of March, and in the night-time, without regard to any winds; it's always invisible, except in the night, being all day either abroad at fishing, or all the day underground upon its nest, which it digs very far under ground. . . The young puffin is fat as the young fulmar, and goes away in August if its first egg be spar'd. . .

. . . The scraber, so called in St Kilda; in the Farn Islands, puffinet; in Holland, the Greenland dove; its bill small, sharp pointed, a little crooked at the end, and prominent; it is as large as a pigeon, its whole body being black, except a white spot on each wing; its egg grey, sharp at one end, blunt at the other. . .

The east coast of Scotland is not a happy hunting ground for island collectors. For all its miles of coastline it can boast only one island worthy of the name – the Isle of May. Yes, there are a few little gems of islets (islands less than forty hectares in area by my definition) such as Inchkeith, Inchcolm, and the Bass Rock, but only one *island*, and even it is only forty-five hectares (111 acres) in area. Nevertheless, it has so much of interest to offer that it puts many a larger island to shame.

The early Vikings recognised its prolific birdlife – herring gulls, fulmar, shag, kittiwake, guillemot, razorbill and puffin (but no gannets) – and they named it Gull Island (*maa-øy*). But they cared less for the human occupants and in 870 murdered Adrian, the first Bishop of St Andrews, with his followers when he was attempting to find shelter. He was buried on the island which soon became a celebrated place of Christian pilgrimage with its own Priory and other religious buildings. These are now the subject of an ongoing archaeological investigation.

David I, who was Henry I of England's brother-in-law, built a chapel dedicated to St Adrian and then presented the island to an English Benedictine Order, but about twenty years later (c.1270) Alexander III persuaded the Archbishop of St Andrews to buy it back secretly as he was worried that it might give the English control of the Firth of Forth. Certainly, when news of the sale became public, the English immediately tried to rescind it. The Pope was petitioned and time dragged on until, finally, Bannockburn settled the issue.

The English navy's reaction was to move in and flatten the Priory, which was by that time one of the kingdom's wealthiest establishments, and for the next few centuries whenever anything worthwhile was built on the island the English came along and destroyed it. Even so, St Adrian's (wrecked) shrine continued to be a popular place of pilgrimage and among the many notable visitors were Mary of Gueldres, *en route* from the Netherlands in 1449 to marry James II, and James IV, who made several pilgrimages.

We anchored at Altarstones which was sheltered from the wind and used the rusty iron steps to climb ashore but there was such a swell that our inflatable dinghy kept crashing against the sharp limpets on the rocks. In the the end we had to manhandle it up to higher ground.

The May has always been a serious shipping hazard and the area round it is littered with wrecks. So, about 1630, an entrepreneur called Alexander Cunningham, bought the island and obtained permission to erect and maintain 'ane Lighthous' on the 'yle of Maij' and to charge an 'impost' on passing ships to pay for it. The lighthouse he built was a simple platform, twelve metres high, on which a fire was kept burning every night and it was Scotland's very first lighthouse.

Cunningham's son, John, together with James Maxwell, obtained official Parliamentary approval in 1645 to improve the design of 'The Beacon' by raising the platform to eighteen metres and enclosing it like a Border keep. The architect for this unusual building was drowned when his boat capsized during a supervision visit. Several old ladies of Pittenweem were blamed for the tragedy and burned as witches.

The impost – four Scots shillings a ton for foreign ships and two shillings for home vessels – was collected by Customs officers on the Fife coast. It brought in about £280 sterling per year (about £100,000 in today's money). The light came from burning a ton of coal each night in a grate or 'chauffer' at the top of the tower but in gale winds up to three tons of coal could be consumed.

The lighthouse was rather unsatisfactory, particularly as in a storm very little light could be seen on the dangerous windward side. There were still many shipwrecks and continual complaints but nothing was done until two Royal Navy frigates, *Pallas* and *Nymph*, were wrecked on the rocks near Dunbar in 1810. The pilots said they thought a limekiln at Broxmouth was the May light, and that the May light was the Bell Rock. At last the Government acted. The Commissioners of Northern Lights bought the island in 1815 for £60,000 and started construction of the present lighthouse – using the very latest design of oil lamps with reflectors.

The two lighthouses are an interesting contrast and only a short distance apart. The new one is now automated but it was still manned when we visited the island and we spent an enjoyable half-hour chatting in the sun with one of the keepers who proudly showed us the fine furniture he had built, his boxes full of books, and his walled vegetable garden by the Loch carefully protected from the rabbits.

By Altarstones, Isle of May

BASS ROCK

Chapel ruin

Castle Ruin

Lighthouse

BASS ROCK

. . . The solan goose is in size somewhat less than a land goose, and of a white colour, except the tips of the wings which are black, and the top of their head which is yellow; their bill is long, small pointed, and very hard, and pierces an inch deep into wood, in their descent after a fish laid on a board, as some use to catch them. When they sleep they put their head under their wings, but one of them keeps watch, and if that be surprised by the fowler all the rest are then easily caught. . . but if the sentinel gives warning, by crying loud, then all the flock make their escape. When this fowl fishes for herring it flies about sixty yards high, and then descends perpendicularly into the sea, but after all other fish it descends a-squint; the reason for this manner of pursuing the herrings is, because they are in greater shoals than any other fish whatsoever. . .

It is interesting to compare those two great volcanic rock-plugs, Ailsa Craig in the Firth of Clyde and the Bass Rock in the Firth of Forth. Ailsa Craig is very much the larger of the two – more than twelve times the area and three times the height with all the assets of an impregnable fortress – yet history has been relatively kind and we talk of it amiably as 'Paddy's Milestone' or the 'fairy rock'. The Bass Rock, on the other hand, has a dour history of war and imprisonment and no friendly epithets.

There are no gannets on the nearby Isle of May yet the Bass Rock is crowded with them to such an extent that when the gannet was no longer being called the 'solan goose' it took its Latin name from the Bass Rock – *Morus bassanus*.

There have been only two long-term owners in historical times. The Lauder family, later known as the Lauders of the Bass, were granted ownership by Malcolm Canmore in 1056 and they probably built the fortifications which were first mentioned in 1405. Then in 1706 ownership passed to Sir Hew Dalrymple, and it is his descendent Sir Hew Hamilton-Dalrymple who still owns it today.

From the mainland the Bass Rock appears to slope gradually down to the sea but it is in fact divided into three rough terraces. The lowest terrace has two landing places below the lighthouse but landing is never easy because of the continual swell. The remains of the fortress/prison are at this level. On the second terrace are the ruins of St Baldred's Chapel, probably built on the site of his original anchorite cell. He was an Irish missionary who died in 606 and he may have been the first inhabitant. The highest terrace has the remains

The Bass Rock – guardian of the Forth

of a walled vegetable garden and the island's only source of fresh water – little more than a catchment area for surface water.

The turbulent history of the Bass Rock drew to a close with a swashbuckling adventure in the best of vintage Hollywood traditions. When Charles II had been restored as monarch in 1660 he set out to destroy the power of the Church of Scotland. The Covenanters fought back with secret 'conventicles', but so many were arrested that in 1671 the fortress on the Bass Rock was purchased by the Government to use as a state prison for the rebellious Presbyterians. Seventeen years later, when James VII was relieved of the Crown and William of Orange proclaimed king, the imprisoned Presbyterians were released although the garrison on the Bass Rock and much of Scotland remained faithful to James. This support was slowly eroded until after the Battle of Killiecrankie the only remaining Jacobite stronghold left in the whole of Scotland was the Bass Rock. Under its Governor, Sir Charles Maitland, it held out for nearly two years but was eventually starved into submission in 1690.

It was then the turn of the Presbyterians to imprison four young Jacobites on the Bass Rock. But not for long. In June 1691 a regular supply ship laden with coal arrived at the Rock. The Prison Governor, Fletcher of Saltoun, and some of his garrison were on the mainland at the time so the remaining guards went down to the landing place to help unload the ship. While they were there the four prisoners escaped from their cells, closed and barred the prison gates, and turned the guns on the guards outside, ordering them to leave the island. After they had taken control, the four young men were joined by one of the ex-garrison's gunners and sixteen of their friends from East Lothian. With the support of an occasional shipload of provisions from France this small group held the strategic Bass Rock on behalf of the Jacobites for nearly four years!

In the end, the exasperated British Government had to set up a naval blockade in order to force the Jacobites to surrender or face starvation and, sure enough, on the 18th of April 1694 a flag of truce appeared on the Rock. Major Reid was sent over by the Privy Council to deliver the terms of capitulation. The rebels, looking very relaxed, insisted that the Major should join them for a meal. Using their last remaining stocks, a huge feast was produced with bottles of the finest French wine and brandy. The men treated the food with such abandon that by the end of the meal the Major was convinced that they must have limitless supplies. Unconditional surrender it seemed was not an option and only the terms of a possible truce were of interest.

After discussions ashore the rebels were granted complete indemnity for 'life, liberty, and fortune', an honourable surrender, and freedom either to remain in Scotland or take passage to France at Government expense.

Following this event a chastened Government dismantled the fortress.

Appendix of relevant maps and charts

Ailsa Craig OS Maps: 1:50000 Sheet 76 1:25000 Sheet 490 1:10000 (NX 09)
Admiralty Chart: 1:75000 No.2126

Sanda OS Maps: 1:50000 Sheet 68 1:25000 Sheet 489
Admiralty Charts: 1:75000 No.2126 or 2199

Texa OS Maps: 1:50000 Sheet 60 1:25000 Sheet 439
Admiralty Chart: 1:75000 No.2168

Cara OS Maps: 1:50000 Sheet 62 1:25000 Sheet 426
Admiralty Chart: 1:25000 No.2475

Gigha OS Maps: 1:50000 Sheet 62 1:25000 Sheet 426
Admiralty Charts: 1:75000 No.2168 1:25000 No.2475

Oronsay OS Maps: 1:50000 Sheet 61 1:25000 Sheet 375
Admiralty Charts: 1:75000 No.2169

Eileach an Naoimh OS Maps: 1:50000 Sheet 55 1:25000 Sheet 354 and 365
Admiralty Charts: 1:75000 No.2169 1:25000 No.2386

Scarba OS Maps: 1:50000 Sheet 55 1:25000 Sheet 365
Admiralty Charts: 1:25000 No.2326 or 2343

Eilean Righ OS Maps: 1:50000 Sheet 55 1:25000 Sheet 365
Admiralty Chart: 1:25000 No.2326

Luing OS Maps: 1:50000 Sheet 55 1:25000 Sheets 354 and 365
AdmiraltyCharts:1:75000 No.2169 1:25000 No.2326

Kerrera OS Maps: 1:50000 Sheet 49 1:25000 Sheets 331, 343 and 344
Admiralty Charts: 1:25000 No.2387 1:10000 No.1790

Lismore OS Maps: 1:50000 Sheet 49 1:25000 Sheets 318, 330 and 331
Admiralty Chart: 1:25000 No.2378

Ulva OS Maps: 1:50000 Sheet 47 1:25000 Sheet 328
Admiralty Chart: 1:25000 No.2652

Staffa OS Maps: 1:50000 Sheet 48 1:25000 Sheet 328
Admiralty Charts: 1:25000 No.2652 or 2771

Lunga OS Maps: 1:50000 Sheet 46 or 48 1:25000 Sheet 315
Admiralty Charts: 1:75000 No.2171 1:25000 No.2652

Gunna OS Maps: 1:50000 Sheet 46 1:25000 Sheet 300
Admiralty Charts: 1:75000 No.2171 Sound of Gunna 1:25000 No.2475

Coll OS Maps: 1:50000 Sheet 46 1:25000 Sheets 286 and 300
Admiralty Charts: 1:100000 No.1796 1:75000 No.2171

Muck OS Map: 1:50000 Sheet 39 1:25000 Sheet 274
Admiralty Charts: 1:100000 No.1796 1:50000 No.2207

Eigg OS Maps: 1:50000 Sheet 39 1:25000 Sheet 261
Admiralty Chart: 1:100000 No.1796 1:50000 No.2207

Rum OS Maps: 1:50000 Sheet 39 1:25000 Sheets 233 and 261
Admiralty Charts: 1:100000 No.1796 1:50000 Nos.2207 and 2208

Canna OS Maps: 1:50000 Sheet 39 1:25000 Sheet 232
Admiralty Charts: 1:100000 No.1795 or 1796

Berneray OS Maps: 1:50000 Sheet 31 1:25000 Sheet 260
Admiralty Charts: 1:100000 No.1796 1:30000 No.2769

Mingulay OS Maps: 1:50000 Sheet 31 1:25000 Sheet 260
Admiralty Charts: 1:100000 No.1796 1:30000 No.2769

Barra OS Maps: 1:50000 Sheet 31 1:25000 Sheets 231 and 247
Admiralty Charts: 1:100000 No.1796 1:30000 No.2769 and 2770

Hellisay OS Maps: 1:50000 Sheet 31 1:25000 Sheet 231
Admiralty Charts: 1:100000 No.1796 1:30000 No.2770

Eriskay OS Maps: 1:50000 Sheet 31 1:25000
Sheets 216 and 231
Admiralty Charts: 1:100000 No.1795 1:30000 No.2770

Monachs OS Maps: 1:50000 Sheet 22 1:25000 Sheet 135
Admiralty Charts: 1:200000 No.2722

Hirta OS Maps: 1:50000 Sheet 18 1:25000 Sheet 1373
Admiralty Charts: 1:500000 No.2635 1:200000 No.2721

Boreray OS Maps: 1:50000 Sheet 18 1:25000 Sheet 1373
Admiralty Charts: 1:500000 No.2635 1:200000 No.2721

Scarp OS Maps: 1:50000 Sheet 13 1:25000 Sheet 88
Admiralty Charts: 1:200000 No.2721 1:50000 No.2841

Taransay OS Maps: 1:50000 Sheet 18 1:25000
Sheets 98 and 107
Admiralty Charts: 1:200000 No.2721 1:50000 No.2841

Berneray (Sound of Harris) OS Maps: 1:50000 Sheet 18
1:25000 Sheet 116
Admiralty Charts: 1:100000 No.1795 1:20000 No.2642
(part only)

The Shiants OS Maps: 1:50000 Sheet 14 1:25000 Sheet 108
Admiralty Charts: 1:100000 No.1794 or 1795

Isay OS Maps: 1:50000 Sheet 23 1:25000 Sheet 153
Admiralty Charts: 1:100000 No.1795 1:25000 No.2533

Soay OS Maps: 1:50000 Sheet 32 1:25000 Sheet 217
Admiralty Chart: 1:50000 No.2208

The Crowlins OS Maps: 1:50000 Sheet 24 or 32 1:25000
Sheet 188
Admiralty Charts: 1:50000 No.2209 1:25000 No.2498

Raasay OS Maps: 1:50000 Sheet 24 1:25000
Sheets 171 and 187 – and for the extreme north,
Sheets 154,155 and 172
Admiralty Charts: 1:50000 Nos.2209 and 2210

Rona (South) OS Maps: 1:50000 Sheet 24 1:25000 Sheet 155
Admiralty Chart: 1:500000 No.2210

Tanera Beg OS Maps: 1:50000 Sheet 15 1:25000 Sheet 101
Admiralty Charts: 1:100000 No.1794 1:25000 No.2501

Handa OS Maps: 1:50000 Sheet 9 1:25000 Sheet 61
Admiralty Charts: 1:100000 No.1785 1:25000 No.2503

Rona (North) OS Maps: 1:50000 Sheet 8 1:25000 Sheet 39
Admiralty Charts: 1:200000 No.1954 1:25000 No.2524

Foula OS Maps: 1:50000 Sheet 4 1:25000 Sheet 18
Admiralty Charts: 1:75000 No.3283 1:75000 No.3281
NE part only

Vaila OS Maps: 1:50000 Sheets 3 and 4 1:25000 Sheet 16
Admiralty Charts: 1:75000 No.3283 or 3281 1:25000 No.3295

Papa Stour OS Maps: 1:50000 Sheet 3 1:25000
Sheet 13
Admiralty Charts: 1:75000 No.3281

Unst OS Maps: 1:50000 Sheet 1 1:25000 Sheets 1, 2 and 4
Admiralty Chart: 1:75000 No.3282

Fetlar OS Maps: 1:50000 Sheet 1 or 2 1:25000 Sheet 5
Admiralty Charts: 1:75000 No.3282 1:30000 No.3292 west
part

Mousa OS Maps: 1:50000 Sheet 4 1:25000 Sheet 20
Admiralty Charts: 1:200000 No.1119 1:75000 No.3283

Fair Isle OS Maps: 1:50000 Sheet 4 1:25000 Sheet 22
Admiralty Charts: 1:25000 No.2622

Eday OS Maps: 1:50000 Sheet 5 1:25000
Sheets 24, 27 and 30
Admiralty Charts: 1:200000 No.1942 or 1954 1:75000
No.2250

Sanday OS Maps: 1:50000 Sheet 5 1:25000 Sheets 25 and 27
Admiralty Charts: 1:200000 No.1942 or 1954 1:75000
No.2250

Hoy OS Maps: 1:50000 Sheet 7 1:25000 Sheets 33 and 36
Admiralty Charts: 1:200000 No.1954
– 1:75000 No.2249 north Hoy 1:50000 No.2162 south Hoy

Isle of May OS Maps: 1:50000 Sheet 59 1:25000 Sheet 364
Admiralty Charts: 1:75000 No.175 or 190 1:25000 No.734

Bass Rock OS Maps: 1:50000 Sheet 66 1:25000 Sheet 396
Admiralty Charts: 1:75000 No.175 1:50000 No.734